ADVANCE

Sheryl Ramstad has written a book filled with wisdom about the power of learning how to survive in the face of unimaginable adversity. She takes us from the thrill of her first solo airplane flight to the horrors of the burn unit where she ended up in her journey. But that was just the beginning of Sheryl's lifelong quest to find meaning in a life upended by the unexpected. I found it fascinating to follow Sheryl from her physical recovery to her determination to fill each day with a new adventure in business, on the bench, back to school, and even to the top of a mountain. It's a story that is sure to inspire you to continue putting one foot in front of the other no matter what obstacles we all may face.

Pat Miles, Scottsdale, Arizona. Author of *Before All is Said and Done*, Hall of Fame Broadcaster, former TV news anchor and radio journalist.

This inspiring memoir is one Wow moment after another. I was in near tears and filled with joy and cheer as I read how the author's near-death experience heightened her deep understanding of and compassion for others. Her description of the airplane crash she narrowly survived, the challenges of burn treatment and therapy, and the long road to recovery made it hard to put this book down. After the crash, Sheryl was on a quest both to overcome a sense of fragility and to test her self-doubt by remarkable achievements. After having had an impressive career as a trial lawyer, judge, and mediator, she returned to college at age 62 to attain a doctorate in nursing practice and went back to the burn unit where this story began, providing a path for her to give back to others and to evidence the gratitude she felt for her survival. This memoir was beautifully written, and I thoroughly enjoyed reading it.

Eileen Engel, M.D., Erie, Pennsylvania. Emergency Medicine Specialist.

This page turning tour de force is a gripping account of a young woman's life-changing ordeal when a near-fatal plane crash on her first solo flight as a student pilot transformed her world in an instant. Sheryl Ramstad's compelling memoir takes readers on a breathtaking journey through harrowing and transformative experiences as she faced a bleak prognosis, unimaginable pain, numerous surgeries, extensive burns, and an unbelievable recovery. Despite overwhelming odds, her tenacity and unwavering faith became lifelines. More than merely surviving, Sheryl redefined life on her own terms. Readers will walk alongside in her moments of struggle and victory and be inspired by her resolve to rebuild a meaningful, fulfilling life after losing everything except her resilience.
Professor Owen L. Anderson, Georgetown, Texas. University of Texas School of Law.

Sheryl Ramstad has written a riveting account of her tumultuous and impassioned life. Her accomplishments, especially after her catastrophic plane crash, are astonishing. Revealing her story in an enthralling fashion, readers will be emboldened by her courage, her determination to heal, and her contributions to the lives of others. *Living Life Full Throttle* is at once horrifying, provocative, and illuminating, and it's a story that demands to be read.
Janet Horvath, St. Paul, Minnesota. Award winning author of *The Cello Still Sings—A Generational Story of the Holocaust and of the Transformative Power of Music,* **Minnesota Orchestra's associate principal cello 1980-2012, national speaker, and contributor to numerous national and international publications.**

An accomplished and fiercely independent trial lawyer, Sheryl Ramstad was no stranger to high-stakes challenges. Yet, her fortitude was put to the ultimate test when the near-fatal plane crash on her first solo flight as a student pilot resulted in severe burns to over one-third of her body and complications that caused doctors to give her less than a one percent chance of survival. With unwavering grit, she pivoted to a new career, raised a family, ran her state's prisons, and served in Governor Jesse Ventura's Cabinet, all while pursuing new feats of endurance and adventure—running several marathons and climbing one of the world's highest peaks. From the depths of despair, she discovered new strengths—not only to survive but to flourish. Reading this account of Sheryl Ramstad's emotional highs, lows, tragedies, and triumphs was an extraordinary experience.

Honorable Mary Muehlen Maring, Scottsdale, Arizona. Retired Supreme Court Justice.

Living Life Full Throttle

Surviving, Serving, and Summiting

A Memoir

Sheryl Ramstad

Copyright © 2025 Sheryl Ramstad

All rights reserved. No part of this publication may be reproduced, distributed, or transmitted in any form or by any means, including photocopying, recording or other electronic or mechanical methods, without the prior written permission of the author, except in the case of brief quotations embodied in reviews and certain other non-commercial uses permitted by copyright law.

Without in any way limiting the author's (and publisher's) exclusive rights under copyright, any use of this publication to "train" generative artificial intelligence (AI) technologies to generate text is expressly prohibited. The author reserves all rights to license uses of this work for generative AI training and development of machine learning language models.

Printed in the United States of America

Hardcover ISBN: 978-1-960876-81-2

Paperback ISBN: 978-1-960876-80-5

Library of Congress Cataloging-in-Publication: 2025931823

TABLE OF CONTENTS

CHAPTER 1 The Crash 1

CHAPTER 2 The Long Road To Recovery 25

CHAPTER 3 At Death's Door Again 49

CHAPTER 4 Homecoming 63

CHAPTER 5 Life's A Marathon 85

CHAPTER 6 Valuing Family 107

CHAPTER 7 Committed To Healing 135

CHAPTER 8 When Losing Is Winning 165

CHAPTER 9 Ain't No Mountain High Enough 199

CHAPTER 10 Giving Back 237

EPILOGUE 259

ACKNOWLEDGMENTS 263

CHAPTER 1

The Crash

On a sidewalk next to St. Vincent's Catholic Church in St. Paul, Minnesota, are the charred remains of my body. Twenty feet away lies the twisted burning wreckage of my Piper Tomahawk. I'm barely clinging to life. The fiery crash moments ago has left no part of me untouched; my hair, my face, my hands, my arms, my back, and my legs are on fire. Everything is raw. Searing pain grips me from my face down to the soles of my feet.

A crowd has gathered around, staring at what remains of the smoldering airplane I'd just flown.

Profound silence permeates the air while onlookers stand frozen in shock and disbelief.

Their faces reflect a mixture of horror, pity, and helplessness, as they back away from the unfathomable devastation and destruction playing out before their eyes.

From the heavy wooden doors of the church a priest emerges, his black collar and robe lending an air of solemnity to the already somber situation. In his hands, he holds a small notebook, a symbol of his vocation and his duty to guide the faithful through life's most challenging events. Despite the grisly state I'm in, I see him approach determinedly, conveying that time is of the essence.

With compassion in his eyes, the priest kneels beside me, disregarding the searing heat still radiating from my body. "Are you Catholic?" he says in a soft voice. "May I administer your last rites?" Unsure what difference it makes if I'm Catholic, I reply, "I'm not Catholic, but I would appreciate your prayers." In the commotion, there are so many voices that I don't know what the priest says after that. I know that the sacrament of the last rites is a solemn ritual intended to provide comfort and spiritual support in the face of impending death. The priest makes the weight of the situation clear to me as he seeks to ensure that my departing soul finds solace in the embrace of heaven, while life slips away from me.

In that unsettling moment, I understand how closely life and death can coexist and the fine line between the two. The priest's presence and steadfast dedication to his faith demonstrate the enduring power of compassion in the face of overwhelming tragedy. The gathering crowd looks on. Their collective silence suggests that they, too, recognize the fragility of life and the inevitability of mortality.

Four and a half hours north of where I've collapsed, my day began with a different energy and anticipation. I'd returned to my parents' lake home in Detroit Lakes, Minnesota, after an intense morning run along the shores of Big Floyd Lake. Sweat dripped down my forehead as I made my way back to the house.

Feeling invigorated yet in need of a cool down, I leapt into the refreshing waters of the lake. My husband, Chuck, was returning soon from getting gas for the car to drive us back to our home in St. Paul. The crystal-clear depths momentarily helped me leave behind the worries and stresses of everyday life. Emerging from the water, I felt a renewed sense of vitality, as if the lake itself had washed away any lingering fatigue from my run.

On the afternoon of July 7, 1979, as Chuck and I began our long drive back to the Twin Cities, my mind wandered to a conversation I had with my mother the day before. We'd sat on the dock, drinking our morning coffee, a ritual we never missed when I visited, and we'd admired the reflections in the glassy water. "Honey," Mom said, pushing her ever-present, oversized sunglasses higher on her nose. "I'm concerned about your flying. It worries me. Something might happen to you."

I turned my head so she wouldn't see me roll my eyes, her fretting as ever present as her sunglasses. "You worry too much. The chances of dying in a car accident or by crossing the street are much greater than being killed in an airplane crash. You know I'm always careful. Please don't manufacture something out of whole cloth."

Just then, a mother loon with chicks on her back swam by on the tranquil lake. "Well, dear, I love you deeply and don't know what I'd do if something ever happened to you."

Mom looked so vulnerable sitting there in her white shorts and coral knit top. I hated to be the cause of her anxiety, but I knew if it wasn't this, she'd find something else to consume her thoughts. Still, in that moment, I wanted to comfort her. I touched her bare shoulder. "Don't worry, Mom, I'll be just fine."

Chuck shares my passion for flying, a dream we've both nurtured for the three years of our marriage. Having been a pilot himself since the age of sixteen, he understands the thrill of soaring through the skies. Our dream has been that I would earn my pilot's license so I can become his co-pilot. Together, we envisioned a future where we would have our own plane and use it for leisurely escapes and exciting vacations.

I didn't reveal to Mom that the next day holds a significant milestone for me as an aspiring pilot. I'm scheduled for my first solo flight at a small airfield near our St. Paul home, a rite of passage for any new aviator. After countless hours of training and instruction, the time has come for me to take control of the aircraft entirely on my own.

Excitement and trepidation course through my body as I anticipate the impending event. The freedom and exhilaration of navigating the airspace without an instructor by my side are enthralling prospects. I love soaring through the skies, looking at the landscapes, the streets, the buildings, and the fields below, evoking a sense of wonder and awe within me—a feeling that I'm connected to something greater than myself. To witness the world from a different vantage point isn't just about physically moving through the air; it's about mentally expanding my horizons and embracing the unfamiliar. Yet, the weight of being solely responsible for the safety of the flight also fuels apprehension within me.

On my way home, as the miles roll by, I compose my to-do list of everything I intend to get done after my first solo flight. I map out every minute of my day and evening so that I can accomplish everything I have to do—go to the gym, get groceries, work on a file, and plan for an upcoming meeting. The tasks are listed by the number of minutes each should take, as well as the start and end times. My life boils down to a series of lists to make sure that each hour of every day is productive. By the end of the day, after completing everything on my to-do lists, I'm satisfied knowing that I've managed to accomplish my goals. Occasionally, I remind myself that I need to strike a balance between productivity and maintaining flexibility to enjoy the present moments. I ponder the ongoing struggle to find that balance as I tuck the list in my purse to have it handy when the flight is over but continue to believe that my most crucial task is to complete everything on my to-do list.

    I mentally fortify myself for the significant step I'm about to take. The hum of the car's engine reminds me of the rhythm of the airplane's propeller idling at Homan Field. The distance between my parents' lake home and the Twin Cities mirrors the gulf between my present self and the pilot I'm destined to become. The landscape blurs. Despite my mother's concerns, I've been working toward this moment that will define me and mark the beginning of a new chapter in my life as a pilot.

    After arriving in St. Paul, I drop off my overnight bag and swiftly change into something casual for my aviation adventure. Chuck announces, "I'm staying home. This is your day, and all the attention should be on you. I'll get a bottle of champagne so we can celebrate your solo flight when you return home." Comfortably dressed, I hop into my car. The cloudless, robin's-egg blue sky, the temperature hovering around 80 degrees, the radiant glow of the sun—it's perfect flying weather.

    The small airfield situated on the outskirts of St. Paul is a half-hour drive from my home. When I approach, the vibrant scene of small planes taking off and landing greets my eyes. Their wings gracefully cut through the air, showcasing the essence of aviation. The atmosphere pulses with energy, and the odor of fuel and the hum of engines fill the air. My eagerness to embark on this milestone journey heightens.

After parking in the designated area, I step out of the car and walk to the registration building. My flight instructor is waiting for me. He greets me with a warm smile, enthusiastically expresses confidence in my abilities, and outlines the plan for my solo flight. We'd take off together, fly the designated flight pattern, and return to the airport. He'd then get out of the plane and relinquish the controls to me.

My solo flight would involve performing three *touch-and-goes*. The maneuver consists of flying a rectangular flight pattern, descending toward the ground during the final approach, briefly touching the runway, and swiftly ascending again to repeat the sequence. I'd showcase my skills while executing this sequence three times. With the third touchdown, I'd bring the aircraft to a halt and taxi back to the airport. My flight instructor would be waiting for me there, marking the conclusion of my first solo flight.

True to his word, after flying the pattern together, my instructor gets out of the aircraft, leaving me alone in the cockpit. The weight of the moment settles upon me, and the freedom and independence of flying solo are now a reality.

Air traffic is intense. It is a holiday weekend. With a deep breath and a surge of determination, I prepare to do my three *touch-and-goes*. The nervous anticipation and sheer excitement create a whirlwind of emotions. Each maneuver requires precision and focus to navigate the aircraft through the designated flight pattern. Although flying solo thrills me, the responsibility is daunting.

When the engine roars to life, a surge of adrenaline washes over me. The radio crackles with instructions. The final checks completed, I take a deep breath and taxi down the runway, each turn and movement reminding me of the countless hours of training that had brought me to this point. Once the control tower grants me clearance, my hands tighten around the controls. Pushing forward on the throttle, the aircraft accelerates down the runway, and its wheels leave the ground. An indescribable sensation of liberation grips me. The world falls away beneath me as I soar higher into the sky, leaving behind any doubts or fears that accompany me on the ground.

A newfound confidence blossoms within me. The steady drone of the engine and the wind whistling past the wings create a symphony of sounds that fills my ears. I am both empowered and humbled; I'm solely in charge of the aircraft's movements. As I maneuver through the sky, the landscape unfolds below like a breathtaking canvas—the patchwork of city streets, the meandering Mississippi River, and the panoramic view of downtown St. Paul. I marvel at the beauty of the world from this unique perspective, feeling a sense of connection to the pioneers of flight who came before me.

Throughout the flight, I experience a feeling of accomplishment at each turn, climb, and descent. The minutes fly by, and before I know it, I've made two *touch-and-goes*. My heart races in anticipation of my third and final maneuver, which will complete my first solo flight as a student pilot. I'm confident in my abilities, and the control tower clears me for landing.

Flying over the bustling cityscape, with the Mississippi River, I-94, and the Minnesota State Capitol in view, the plane's engine abruptly refuses to respond and sputters intermittently. Time slows, and my heart freezes in my chest when the dire situation hits me with full force. I radio the air traffic control tower for assistance. "The engine's sputtering. Help! I can't stop it!"

Then the engine quits. The aircraft begins to descend, plummeting through the sky like a free-falling lead weight. The absence of the engine's vibration—the complete silence—leaves a void in the cockpit. The once majestic aircraft could crumble at any moment. As the plane rapidly descends, my mind whirls to find a solution. I hear the control tower directing other planes to clear the airspace for me. Below, I-94 bustles with heavy traffic on that July 4th weekend, and the Mississippi River is filled with hundreds of boats enjoying the sunny holiday afternoon. Nearby, the Minnesota State Capitol and densely populated residential neighborhoods stand as stark reminders of the collateral damage, perhaps deaths, I could cause. Somehow I have to avoid them. Although it takes less than thirty seconds for the plane to go down, every second feels like an eternity. I desperately search for somewhere safe to land. No open spaces anywhere. Fearing the potential consequences of the aircraft's impending impact, I resolve not to jeopardize the lives of others.

Gravity seems to intensify. The plane descends, pulling me down with unyielding force. In that terrifying moment, my training and instincts kick in while I struggle to fight paralyzing fear to regain control of the situation. Each passing moment brings the ground closer. I search for any glimmer of hope, scanning the surroundings for a potential spot to land or any sign of assistance. I'd never had training on what I should do if the engine quit other than my instructor hypothetically asking when we were flying over an open field what I'd do if the plane malfunctioned. I knew that instinct leads inexperienced pilots to go full throttle—pulling the throttle back so the nose of the plane gains altitude. But I knew that would be deadly. It would cause the engine to stall. I told my instructor that I'd simply set the nose at landing speed so it wouldn't nosedive into the ground. When the engine quits, that's what I do. But the plane dives, pulling me downward in a freefall. I still can't see any open spaces below. I think I will die, although somehow, crazy as it seems, I hope that I might overcome this seemingly insurmountable challenge.

Holding tightly to the controls, I stay alert. The entire time, I focus on avoiding houses, buildings, cars, a church steeple, the State Capitol, and boats below. As the doomed plane hurtles toward the ground, I spot a vacant playground and aim the nose of the plane toward it. Suddenly I hear the harsh clashing of metal. A power line savagely rips off one of the plane's wings and ignites the fuel, engulfing the cockpit in flames.

Fire threatens to crumple the plane around me and consume me alive. Thick smoke clouds my sight, sharply burning my eyes. With a deafening roar, the plane crashes into a tall tree, tearing through backyards and once-tidy fences and leaving a path of destruction in its wake. The sharp screech of tearing metal reverberates as the crippled aircraft skids to an abrupt stop within ten feet of a woman sunbathing in her backyard.

I know I have to escape the cockpit, or I'll be burned alive. I pull against the latch between the doors, attempting to release it, but nothing happens. The forcefulness of the crash has caused the doors to jam. There's no way out. If I don't do something drastic, I'll die, I think. With a surge of adrenaline and supernatural strength, I throw all my body weight against the far door. The door pops open. I climb through the fire and yell to the crowd that's gathering, "Get away from the plane before it explodes!" I'm terrified the lives of people living in this neighborhood are in jeopardy. Would the fuel tanks blow up? What if the grass catches fire and spreads to neighboring houses?

A man approaches me. "Is anyone still in the plane?"

"No, I'm alone. It's my first solo flight. I don't know what happened."

"I don't know either, but I do know one thing. I'm a commercial pilot. I saw you bring down that incapacitated plane, and you did a damn good job of flying."

The crowd grows. No one says a word. It's as though they're all watching a riveting movie on a theater screen. When the commercial pilot helps me stumble across the street toward St. Vincent's, the people step out of my way as if I'm carrying a contagious disease

I collapse on the sidewalk in front of the church. Burned flesh hangs from my body. When the priest offers me last rites, I feel like the end is near. The air is heavy with disbelief and the acrid smell of fuel. Neighbors continue to emerge from their homes with shocked looks on their faces. I hear someone say there was a whooshing sound before they saw the propeller wasn't spinning and then the plane lost altitude. A big thud shook their houses. How thankful I am that I avoided crashing into them.

I drift in and out of consciousness. The crowd gathers while emergency responders swarm the area, their sirens piercing the air. The ambulance, fire engines, and police cars somehow cut a path through the disorder and chaos. I'm thankful the commercial pilot waits with me until the ambulance pulls up to where I'm lying.

Amidst the commotion, a man steps forward and identifies himself as the St. Paul Fire Chief. "Which hospital would you like to go to?" he asks.

"I have no idea. I've never been in a hospital before."

He tries to assure me. "We have one of the best burn units in the country half a mile from here."

"Please take me there," I gasp.

The Chief asks my name. "Who should we notify?"

"Please call my brother Jim. He'll inform the rest of my family. But please don't contact my parents; let Jim do it."

When the ambulance leaves the crash site, paramedics beside me monitor my vital signs. "May I have some water? I'm so thirsty," I plead.

Neither paramedic responds, but one paramedic says to the other, "Given her extensive burns, I don't know whether she can have water."

The other replies, "Yeah, we'll have to check at the hospital to see what the protocol is." I remember wondering what good it would do for me then.

The ambulance ride makes me feel like extra baggage. Neither paramedic talks to me, much less explains what will happen or the extent of my injuries. I search their eyes for reassurance that I will survive, but they remain focused on each other. I briefly grab the gaze of one of them, seeking answers to questions pounding through my brain. Were these my final moments? I force myself to focus on how I would survive. Then the ambulance arrives at the hospital's emergency entrance, which I hope will be the gateway to my survival.

In a flurry of activity at the hospital entrance, a multitude of medical professionals converge on me. They transfer me onto a specialized stretcher designed to minimize any jostling and further injury. The hospital staff work swiftly to cut the charred remnants of my clothing off my body. It's puzzling when someone announces that a newspaper reporter has arrived, seeking an interview and photographs. The medical team immediately dismisses the reporter. "She's in no condition for an interview."

In the emergency room, the sterile white walls surround me, and the faint buzz of medical equipment fills the air. My mouth feels like I need to brush my teeth. I'm weighed down by a despair so bleak I can barely breathe. The doctors, nurses, and aides talk with one another. None of the conversation is directed my way. I focus on the female doctor, searching her eyes for signs of what is happening to me. I'd never been prone to panic, but I want answers to the question pounding through my brain. I can't help wondering if I'll live through this. I need reassurance. In the tense atmosphere, in my dazed state, I fade in and out of consciousness. When I try to speak, no words come out. The nurses scurry to hook me up to all sorts of monitors and give me drugs intravenously. I have no idea what they will do next or where I will end up. I'm completely at their mercy.

A scuffling sound on the other side of the screen catches my attention. In bursts my brother Jim, eyes frantic, his face drained of color. I try to apologize for causing him to leave his July 4th party at his lake home, but I can't speak. My body feels numb, the painkillers at work. His panicky eyes scan my battered body. Looking for signs of hope, I only see anguish behind Jim's gentle smile. "Mom and Dad are on their way. They chartered a plane and should be here shortly. Chuck is waiting for them at the airport. He'll bring them to you as soon as they land."

Jim appears helpless. His eyes, normally bright and full of life, are clouded with worry as he stands at my bedside, his demeanor in the face of my pain causing me even greater discomfort. He says, "I better go now so the medical people can take care of you." His voice falters. As he turns to leave, I can see a mix of reluctance to leave and the need to escape the situation he can do nothing about. Honestly, I'm relieved when he leaves. Overwhelmed with trying to keep my own fears at bay, I don't need his, too.

The physical and emotional toll of the ordeal taking hold, I'm immersed in a state of shock. My consciousness fades and time blurs. When I do wake up, I find myself in a room I share with three other patients on the burn unit. At my bedside stand my parents, their faces exhausted and concerned. "We love you, Sheryl. We're here for you," Mom says trying to hold back her tears. "You're so strong, honey. You'll come through this. You're not alone. Many prayers are being said for you." Dad stands lifelessly behind Mom.

Then Chuck tenderly touches the top of my head. "Sheryl, you did an amazing job of landing that plane without killing anyone," he says. "I'm proud of you."

Mom turns away to wipe her tears. She takes a nearby chair and announces, "I'm staying with you all night."

Like Jim, Dad doesn't do well in hospitals. A man of few words, he says he'll find a hotel room. "I'll help your father," Chuck offers. When he and Dad leave the hospital, I doze off. A few hours later, I wake up to see Mom asleep in the chair, a Bible in her lap. I feel reassured by her presence, knowing that she'll be my advocate and remain by my side. I remember her comment about my strength and what it would mean to my survival. I recall how she'd brought me up—to fear nothing and believe in my ability to conquer any challenge that came my way. I realize that no medical professional could tell me whether I'd survive the crash. It might take every bit of willpower and determination to recover from my injuries, but I would do it.

Before the crash, my life was meticulously orchestrated, each day a carefully balanced act of efficiency and productivity. I planned my days obsessively, starting with a morning run to ensure both my mental and physical sharpness, and then transitioning into a whirlwind of professional rigor. The courtroom was my arena. As a criminal lawyer, trying cases was not just a job but a calling. Every argument made and every question asked was a step toward the truth. The intensity was exhilarating, and I thrived on the challenges, always striving for a fair and just outcome. Even after the office had emptied, my days were far from over. Invariably the last person to leave, my arms laden with files to work on, home became an extension of my office. The lines between work and personal life blurred, but it was a choice I willingly made. Not a minute wasted, I juggled responsibilities, pushing the limits of what could be achieved in a single day. The endless stream of work was not a burden but a badge of honor, a tangible measure of my belief that I could make a difference in the world, one case at a time.

I could never have anticipated how my life would change. In the hospital, the days seem to belong to someone else. My vibrant world before this ordeal, filled with the hustle of busy days, feels irrelevant in the face of my current reality, replaced by the clinical ambiance of the burn unit. I'm thrust into a bewildering world that is largely incomprehensible. The terminology, the procedures, and the reality of my condition feel alien, as if I'd been dropped into a parallel universe where everything I know is turned on its head. Trying to make sense of it all is like trying to piece together a puzzle without knowing what the final picture is supposed to look like.

The burn unit's impact is extremely disorienting. My every sense is assaulted by the unfamiliar, every moment a challenge to adapt to this new reality. The constant barrage of sounds, the beeping of machines monitoring vital signs, the distant chatter of medical staff discussing terms and procedures I can't understand, the groans of pain from fellow patients, and the sudden, jarring noise of alarms or urgent calls for assistance heighten my anxiety and my sense of vulnerability. At all hours, day and night, sirens and flashing lights of ambulances pierce through the windows, an ominous chorus heard throughout the unit. Watching the 10 o'clock evening news, I see an accident reported, and within minutes, the very individuals involved in the reports are in beds down the hallway from me. The reality of these situations bridges the gap between distant news stories and the personal tragedies unfolding within our walls. There are hushed voices, too, in the hallways discussing patients transported to the unit who do not survive their injuries.

The air is thick with a distinct, sterile odor that clings to every surface. As newly admitted patients are wheeled by, their severely burned bodies smell like campfires. The odor on the unit is pervasive, infiltrating my nostrils with every breath, a mix of antiseptic solutions and the underlying scent of burnt skin unlike anything I've encountered before. At times, the heavy air is hard to draw into my lungs, hard to expel in exhalation, and the visual stimuli are no less intense. Fluorescent lights overhead cast an unforgiving glow over everything as if seeking to expose every detail, every imperfection of my own damaged skin. The pastel walls, cold and impersonal, add to my alienation. My existence narrows to these foreign sights, sounds, and smells—a transition from a world rich with color and life to a muted existence of clinical sounds and antiseptic smells. It's jarring and a vivid indication of how much has changed.

Amidst the harrowing sights and sounds, the medical staff focuses on their purpose to save lives and alleviate suffering. Interactions with staff, though professional, are conducted with an efficiency that leaves little room for warmth. Their movements precise, their procedures practiced to perfection, are all carried out with an emphasis on minimizing any risk of infection. Even the simplest touch is mediated by gowns and gloves, and masks obscuring facial expressions I long to see. The bandages carefully wrapped around my burns and the pricks of heparin needles in my stomach every four hours to prevent blood clots constantly remind me of the reality of my condition. The clinical contact required for my treatment and the comforting, familiar touch I long for from loved ones, underscore the physical isolation imposed by my injuries. My days, no longer my own, are governed instead by the rhythms of medical care and the unpredictable journey of healing.

The sterile environment, while undoubtedly necessary for healing, has an unexpected effect on me as a patient. I feel more like a specimen in a lab than a person. The lack of sensory stimuli, the absence of familiar comforts, and the constant presence of antiseptic smells make me yearn for the messiness of life outside the hospital walls. Initially, I'm entangled in a struggle, fiercely trying to cling to the familiar life I once lived. At the edge of my bed are case files, brought at my behest by colleagues, yet they remain untouched. My hands, swathed in bandages, refuse to cooperate, and every attempt to move is met with my body's outcry of pain. Questions haunt me. Where is the path back to the life I once knew so well?

As days blend into nights in what seems like an endless loop, I have no choice but to pause. My readily apparent predicament gives rise to daunting questions about my future, my identity, and my very purpose, which loom large over me. The endless passage of time leaves me with no alternative but to confront these challenges head-on. I turn to prayer, not just as a plea for healing, but to connect with a sense of peace and acceptance of my current state. I begin to unravel the real significance of my existence and to reevaluate what truly matters in my life, reshape my values and my perception of self-worth. The existential challenge of my situation becomes all too real as questions overwhelm me. Why me? How had I survived? What am I meant to do with this second chance?

Life had brought me to my knees. Faith became my anchor, a beacon guiding me through the dark moments navigating this new world. The loss of my former self was, in many ways, a shedding of superficial layers, revealing a core strength I had not known existed within me. Trusting in the

Lord to guide me on this journey helped me release the anxiety of the unknown and embrace the present, teaching me the true meaning of humility—surrendering control and trusting in a power greater than myself. As I look back, this was a pivotal chapter in my life where I was molded and strengthened in ways I could never have imagined. There, in the stillness and the struggle, I found a deeper connection to the Lord than I had ever had before.

Firefighters putting out the flames at crash site

Living Life Full Throttle

Aircraft remains after the crash

Sheryl Ramstad

Newspaper photo from the day after the crash (July 8, 1979 -Sunday St. Paul Pioneer Press)

Living Life Full Throttle

Sunday headline story of the airplane crash

CHAPTER 2

The Long Road To Recovery

After that dreadful first day in the burn unit, Doctor Solem broached the subject of the distressing hurdle that lay ahead. I'd need surgery in five days—skin grafting to take care of the extensive burns on the tops and palms of my hands, as well as my fingers, my wrists, and my lower arms. Skin would be transplanted from one part of my body, most likely my abdomen, to other areas where the skin was burned off. It had to be done right away to preserve function in the affected areas.

"Couldn't you take the skin from my body to cover Sheryl's burns?" my mother asked.

"No," Dr. Solem explained. "The skin graft donor sites must be from Sheryl's own body.

Skin cannot be donated by others because it would be rejected as foreign tissue by her immune system. Using her own skin increases the likelihood of successful grafts."

The crisp white hospital sheets beneath me crinkled as I writhed in pain. "Mesh grafts involve making staggered slits in the healthy skin taken from her abdomen so it expands to cover a larger part of the damaged areas." The room's bright lights reflected off his glasses, giving his expression an air of intensity. "The appearance of the graft sites will be different from the surrounding skin."

I winced, picturing the surgeon's scalpel slicing through the healthy skin of my abdomen, then peeling it off and stretching it to cover my burned hands and arms. Mom exclaimed, "How does the new skin adhere to her body? Could there be any complications?"

"The new skin will gradually bond with the underlying tissue and blood supply, facilitating the healing process. The grafts are stapled to the body, and the staples will be removed once the new skin adheres," the doctor replied.

It felt like Dr. Solem was describing a science experiment as he explained the risks associated with the surgery—bleeding, infection, and partial or complete loss of the grafts. "The burns on your right hand extend all the way down to the bone. I'll try to cover them with donor skin, but, truthfully, I don't know if the grafts will take." Then looking directly into my eyes, he continued, "When burns penetrate so deeply, the chances of success are greatly diminished because the lack of adequate blood flow prevents the graft from integrating properly into the surrounding tissues."

He hesitated before saying, "As a trial lawyer, I know you use your hands a lot so it's worth a try. I hope the grafting will be successful. I've seen many so-called miracles in my years here. Often, I think faith has its part to play." I was relieved to know that my doctor was a man of faith. "The recovery will be challenging and extremely painful. You'll need to keep your hands and arms totally immobilized for several days to permit healing. If the grafts do heal sufficiently, physical therapy will be necessary to regain your strength and the function in your hands. If the grafts don't take, I'm sorry to say we'd be looking at the likelihood of amputation."

The doctor's words echoed in my mind. Amputation. Amputation. The thought of the grafts not taking haunted me. What would I do if they failed? The possibility of losing my right hand gripped me with icy fear. My profession requires the use of both hands. I'm right-handed and use it to play tennis and racquetball, activities that keep me physically fit and mentally balanced. I couldn't imagine how I would cope with the loss.

"Do you have any questions?" Dr. Solem asked. I struggled to find words that would rise above the pall in the room. My mind was a whirl of medical terms, potential outcomes, and the unknown that lay ahead. Every scenario that played out in my mind seemed more terrifying than the last.

Apprehensive about delving deeper, afraid of the answers that might come from any questions I dared ask, I still had to fully understand the process and outcomes to prepare myself mentally and emotionally.

Summoning every ounce of courage, I finally opened my mouth to say something. No words came out. I waited a few moments, swallowed hard, and tried again. My voice, hesitant and shaky at first, grew steadier as I asked about the steps of the surgery and the time involved to heal. "How many surgeries will I need?"

"The number of surgeries will depend on how well your burns heal over time and whether you have any complications," he said, looking at me above the rim of his glasses. The doctor's calm demeanor grounded me. "It's still too early to determine the exact course of your treatment. The next 48 hours will tell us a lot. For now, we're prioritizing the worst-affected areas for grafting."

Forty-eight hours? It seemed like a lifetime. "Thank you, Doctor," I said.

He waved me off. "That's my job."

I dreaded enduring multiple surgeries, each with its own set of physical and emotional challenges. The only other time I had undergone the knife was when I had my tonsils out as a three-year-old child. My innocence back then felt worlds apart from the complex reality I now faced. Unlike my previous operation, I was now acutely aware of my grave situation. The upcoming surgery had to be faced head-on if I wanted to regain control of my life and move beyond the scars and pain. Somehow I'd find a way to draw upon the inner reserves of hope and courage that I didn't even know I possessed.

The doctor left me alone with my thoughts in the dimly lit hospital room, the blank walls, utilitarian flooring, crisply uniformed people bustling down wide corridors, the machines and lines and IVs all clustered around me. A medicinal scent hung in the air. The news Dr. Solem delivered reverberated in my mind, refusing to fade away. The emotional pendulum I rode swung between hope and despair, and the quiet didn't help. It was oppressive, amplifying my worries. Then suddenly the door swung open, breaking the silence that enveloped the room. And there she was, Pat, my dear friend, a ray of light among my gloomy thoughts.

Pat, a well-known and beloved news anchor for the local CBS affiliate television station, is my cherished friend. We've shared so many memories. Seeing her standing there reminded me of the life I'd had outside the hospital walls. From the moment Pat and I met, it was as if we'd known each other for a lifetime. We both worked in downtown Minneapolis. During lunchtimes and after work, we took breaks from our demanding professional lives to spend time together. We're close in age—merely a month apart—and have similar passions. We often ran and biked together, and we discussed politics, current events, our families, sports, professional experiences, and our personal challenges. My confidante and the sister I wished for but never had, Pat was a source of unwavering support and understanding. Our connection was deep-rooted and filled a void for me.

She smiled—exactly what I needed at that moment.

"Yesterday was quite a roller coaster, Sheryl." I nodded and indicated she should sit on the bed beside me. "I was getting ready to go on the air for the evening news when the lead story popped up—an airplane crash in a residential area of St. Paul. Crazy, right?" She rubbed her forearms as if chasing away a chill. "There weren't many details. No names had been released. As I read the story, I couldn't shake off the premonition that somehow this story was about you." Pat's voice cracked, and she cleared her throat. "Once I'd wrapped up the newscast, I headed to the hospital emergency room where I thought they'd probably have taken the victims from the crash. Such chaos—doctors, nurses, people rushing around, phones ringing. Then, I spotted your brother Jim. His simple nod was like a gut punch. The terror in his eyes, the frozen face, everything clicked into place. It all added up. You were in that plane crash." I fumbled to put my bandaged arm on Pat's trembling shoulder.

"It's wild, isn't it?" she said. "One minute you're reading news stories like any other day, and the next, you're facing a reality that hits so close to home. I'm trying to make sense of it all. Life's quite a ride, my friend, and sometimes it will throw curve balls. But even through all the madness of this dreadful accident, I'll be here for you, no matter what."

My emotions swelled with gratitude. Despite her apprehension, Pat promised to stand by me. With eyes full of compassion and a calm presence, she slowed my racing thoughts, calming the storm within me. Her silent reassurance reminded me that we'd navigate my recovery together. Promising to return soon, she said, "You need to rest. You've been through a lot."

Shortly after Pat left, my mother approached my bedside, holding the remnants of my charred purse. The acrid odor of burnt leather hit my nostrils. She hesitated for a moment, then spoke softly, "The fire chief dropped these things by the hospital today. They were found at the crash site. He wasn't sure if you wanted them." The purse was barely recognizable, its edges blackened and curling inward. She laid out the contents on a small table next to me—a tube of lipstick twisted into a grotesque shape, a melted compact mirror reflecting a distorted world, a water-logged wallet. Among the ashes and soot, my eyes spotted a singed piece of paper—my to-do list from the day of the crash, filled with mundane tasks—pick up some groceries, go to the gym, work on a file, prepare for a meeting. They'd consumed me just a day earlier. In the whirlwind of daily obligations, each task reminded me of the life I'd been leading, where I was perpetually busy, striving to tick off every box, often burning the candle at both ends until there was nothing left but the flame.

Tears welled up in my eyes. I'd been completely unaware how my life could change in an instant. My body broken and my future uncertain, none of those trivial tasks mattered anymore. Survival was my only concern. The irony was not lost on me—I'd been so driven by the need to accomplish my list, only to find myself now stripped of everything but the sheer will to live.

Mom had been living in Jamestown, North Dakota, before the accident. As soon as I became hospitalized, she moved into a run-down motel across the street from the burn unit. Nothing would interfere with her desire to be with me every step of the way, even an unconventional residence, the closest place she could find to the hospital. The medical staff called her "a force to be reckoned with." Mom was trained as a medical social worker and knew how to strongly advocate for me. Each day, she'd sit by my bedside holding a yellow legal pad and ballpoint pen to jot down every question or concern she had about my care. Anticipating the doctors' arrival early the following morning, she'd position herself outside the men's room. Armed with her pages filled with notes, she'd interrogate them on their way to the restroom.

Every day, she'd ask me, "How much Vivanex have you drunk today? You need to consume the eight pitchers a day the doctor ordered for the protein and calories." How I hated that beverage I was forced to drink even though I knew healing my burns required the nutrients and calories it provided. The smell alone was enough to make my stomach revolt, my gag reflex kicking in as the thick, chalky liquid slid slowly down my throat. It was like drinking liquid plaster. And it tasted even worse—bitter and artificial, leaving an aftertaste that no amount of water could wash away. Consuming just one pitcher first thing each morning seemed like punishment, and then there were still seven more to go. How could something meant to heal me cause such distress?

Mom's unfailing advocacy for my welfare in the burn unit was merely a continuation of the selfless love she'd always shown both my older brother and me. No matter what, she was always there for us. Our biggest cheerleader, she set aside her own career to prioritize our needs. Her voice resonated—steady, reassuring, and filled with an unshakable belief in my ability to recover. While holding my forearm, being careful not to disturb the IV in my arm, she'd say over and over, "Sheryl, you're a strong person. You have what it takes to recover from your injuries. I'll be with you all the way." Through countless long days and sleepless nights, she remained beside me. When I wanted to give up, her determination fueled me. She knew when to encourage me, when to push me to try a little harder. Her belief in my recovery became my own.

From my first day in the burn unit, I tried to pin down the treatment team to find out how long my hospital stay would be. As someone who thrived on setting goals and meeting deadlines, an endless stretch of time felt disconcerting.

Despite the uncertainties about my recovery, I wanted and needed a discharge date. When I asked Dr. Solem about it, he hesitated several minutes. Then he indicated that I'd likely need to be hospitalized at least seven weeks, possibly the entire summer. Counting forward seven weeks from my initial admission, I mentally calculated August 17th, a date I held onto, hell-bent to be liberated on that day.

My only previous experience with burns was when I grabbed a hot pan as a teenager. During my first few days in the burn unit, I learned about the classification system used to categorize burns by different degrees based upon their severity, by their depth into and through the skin.

My face had mostly first-degree burns, which only affected the outer layer of my skin. Despite the constant and stinging pain, these burns were expected to heal with minimal scarring. I was relieved to know that given time, my face would recover without lasting marks. However, the burns on my upper thighs, back, and the undersides of my arms were much more severe. These areas had second-degree burns, which caused damage to both the outer layer of skin and the underlying layer. The intense pain from these burns, the constant blistering, redness, and swelling, made every movement agonizing. The medical team explained that to determine whether or not grafting would be required for my second-degree burns depended upon how well they healed, as each patient's healing process is different.

Third-degree burns are the most severe and always require grafting. These burns affect all layers of the skin, including the deeper tissues, making it impossible for the skin to regenerate naturally. As a result, third-degree burns often lead to significant scarring and permanent tissue damage. The doctors quickly noted the severity of the burns on the tops and palms of my hands, on my fingers and wrists, and on my forearms, indicating that grafting would be essential for those areas. Although my shoulders and upper arms had also suffered third-degree burns much like the rest of my body, immediate grafting would not be possible in those areas because after that surgery, I'd need to be positioned in a way that was not feasible until my hand grafts healed. I'm glad I didn't know how, at that point.

Each morning, Dr. Solem led a procession of professionals into my room, including the head resident, nursing director, occupational and physical therapists, pharmacist, social worker, and chaplain. Armed with clipboards and notebooks, they focused on their tasks, paying little attention to me. Their attention was directed to the details of my treatment, not how I was coping with everything. While undoubtedly well-meaning, their interactions with me seemed detached and clinical, providing minimal feedback, reducing me to a list of symptoms and procedures. I longed for some connection, to know I was not just a case to be managed but a person grappling with pain and fear. Their silence amplified the emotional chasm that seemed to widen with each passing day. When the procession of professionals filed out of my room each morning, I yearned for a touch of empathy amidst the sea of clinical efficiency. Couldn't someone acknowledge the emotional toll of this journey?

My daily routine involved being carted into the "tub room," a space designed for the crucial task of bathing burn patients. The room contained six separate tubs, each occupied by a patient tended to by their bedside nurse. The bathing process stripped me of my very dignity—undoubtedly one of the most distressing and dehumanizing experiences I faced while hospitalized. The bathtubs were placed closely together without any curtains or partitions separating one patient from the next. The lack of privacy caused me immense discomfort.

While the nurses attempted to scrape off the crisply burned skin, my body was exposed and raw, the agony almost unbearable. I tried my best to endure the torment, gritting my teeth as the nurses removed dead tissue to provide fresh, suitable areas for the grafts to be applied. But it felt like the nurses were tearing me apart. Waves of pain radiated through my body. Fellow patients' screams filled the air, a haunting reminder of the immense pain we all endured during this essential yet traumatic procedure. The sounds of their agony created a cacophony of suffering that reverberated in my mind long after the sessions ended. This is what hell must be like, I thought. No inferno could match the agony we experienced in the tub room. Each day, I dreaded the moment I'd be wheeled into that space, knowing the brutal torture that awaited me.

"You should scream, Sheryl! You need to scream to get rid of the pain," the nurses kept telling me. "Let it out." Whatever that meant. As if a few screams could help me. In fact, the opposite was true. The expression of pain didn't help. Only its suppression would guide me through the hard times.

My stoic Norwegian and German heritage prevented me from screaming. Besides, I understood the necessity of enduring these painful processes in order to heal and knew that screams would do nothing to lessen my pain.

"Sheryl, do you want to see a therapist?" the burn doctor asked, his eyes reflecting concern as much as his tone.

"No, I am fine and don't need a therapist," I replied, almost defensively.

I should mention that I majored in psychology and had previously worked with therapists on several psych units. My academic background and professional experience gave me insight into the work of therapists, and I must say, I have my doubts. Talk therapy when addressing profound trauma has its limitations. It seemed to me, their well-intentioned words often floated on the surface, unable to penetrate the deeper layers of a person's suffering. They might offer comfort and coping strategies, but I wondered what they could possibly do for me now that my life had been irrevocably altered. How could a therapist truly relate to the depth of my pain? What relief could they provide that would reach the roots of my distress? This path was distinctly mine to tread. I was determined to marshal my internal resources and endure the healing process in my own way.

During the five days prior to my first grafting, apprehension welled up within me unlike anything I'd experienced before. Being put to sleep filled me with a deep-seated fear. Questions danced in my mind like restless ghosts. How much good skin would be used for the donor sites? Would the grafted areas stand out in stark contrast to the rest of my body? And the nagging question: would the skin graft even take on my hand and if not, what then?

No matter how fervently I wished, I couldn't avoid imminent surgery. A paradoxical blend of emotions churned relentlessly. On the one hand, I wanted the surgery to be done with, for the uncertainty to transform into a tangible reality, no matter what the result might be. On the other hand, contrary to this yearning I had a lingering hope, irrational as it may have been, that somehow, I'd escape the surgery altogether.

Neither the medical team nor my family could quell my panic. Their words couldn't silence the chorus of anxious thoughts that plagued my mind. I was trapped in a whirlwind of "what ifs" that seemed to grow more ominous with each passing hour. When I found myself grappling with the possibility of worst-case scenarios alone at night, the darkness magnified my fears. I laid in bed, staring at the ceiling, feeling the weight of the unknown pressing down on me. The silence was heavy, punctuated only by the soft sounds of the medical equipment around me. During those moments, my questions seemed to multiply, their answers always just out of reach.

Early the morning of my surgery, Mom, Dad, Jim, and Chuck gathered around me, forming a protective circle at my bedside. Dad had flown down from North Dakota to be by my side, juggling the responsibilities of running his business with his steadfast support for my recovery. While Chuck, Mom, and Jim offered words of reassurance, Dad and I shared a silence that spoke volumes—acknowledging the seriousness of my situation.

Fragile and weary, I lay there. Mom tenderly ran her fingers through my hair, then opened her other hand to reveal a small, gleaming object. Her voice was imbued with warmth and a tremor of emotion. "Sheryl, I brought you this gold charm holder on a 14-kt. neck chain." The first charm, a cross, hung there. "I'll continue to add charms as symbols of your recovery."

I looked at the delicate piece, the light catching its intricate details. Mom knew how fond I was of jewelry, how each piece I wore held a story or a memory dear to me. This gift symbolized the hurdles I needed to overcome and the milestones I'd celebrate. Holding the necklace, I felt her love and her heartache. She was not only watching me suffer, she was living it, sharing my pain like only a mother could.

Before the transport team arrived, we recited The Lord's Prayer in unison, the cadence of those familiar words a source of comfort as I entrusted the ultimate outcome to a higher power. The unity of our voices underscored the shared hope that this ordeal would soon be behind us.

The nurses and transport team entered the room. The time had come to say goodbye to my family. They kissed my forehead, their expressions a mix of concern and love, their words laden with well wishes until the last moment. Transport quietly wheeled me through the hospital corridors, leaving me alone with my thoughts. The journey to the operating room felt like an eternity as the future unknowns pressed upon me with renewed intensity. When I finally arrived, the sight of the surgical room's equipment awaited me.

The medical staff went to work, hooking me up to an IV that flowed with anesthetics. When I felt chilled, they draped me with a warm blanket, a small gesture that brought a touch of comfort. As the anesthesia took hold, my consciousness began to fade, and soon I was drifting into a deep slumber.

When I next opened my eyes, I was in the recovery room slowly breaking through the grogginess, and the hushed sounds of medical equipment enveloped me. As the medical personnel ensured my gradual awakening, Dr. Solem appeared, and he said he was pleased with the way the surgery had gone. He reiterated that we'd need to wait to see the ultimate outcome of the graft on my right hand. My family was waiting when I was transported back to my room, their presence soothing as I emerged from the fog of anesthesia. A bit dazed, I mustered the energy to express my relief—it was finally over. My hands and arms were encased in heavy bandages, concealing the grafted areas. My abdomen, which had provided the donor skin, was also wrapped and bandaged, shrouding the visible evidence of the surgery, leaving hope for a successful outcome hanging in the air.

For two weeks following the surgery, the dressings on my hands and arms needed to be removed daily to ensure the new grafts remained moist and securely in place, and splints were applied to immobilize the grafts to prevent them from shifting. The donor sites from my stomach had to be gently washed for proper skin regeneration. At the end of two weeks when the splints were removed, I was extremely relieved to learn that the graft on my right hand was taking.

Once the nurse had removed my dressings, the occupational therapist came to my bedside multiple times each day to work on moving my fingers, hands, and arms to restore and rehabilitate them. My right hand was initially frozen in an extended position, so I was repeatedly encouraged to make a fist. Each time I came a little closer to bending my fingers, I felt a sense of accomplishment and progress. It took countless hours to regain the flexibility in my wrists and a lot of soft tissue work to get those skin grafts to release and move. The therapy sessions were physically demanding and painful, but I needed to endure them for my rehabilitation. Day by day, my hands and arms gradually began moving better; still, it would be a long, slow process to regain function.

It was a good thing there were no mirrors in my hospital room. I was shielded from seeing the full extent of my injuries, likely a deliberate measure to protect patients from the emotional impact of confronting their altered appearances. But for me, not seeing my reflection was both a benefit and a burden; while I was unable to view my changed appearance, I imagined the worst.

Receiving mail played a crucial role in uplifting my spirits—especially one envelope with a photograph of me taken during a ten-kilometer race I'd just run the week before my accident. My parents framed the photo and placed it on the bedstand next to me where it remained throughout my time in the burn unit. It served as a reminder of my capabilities and strength, and bolstered my confidence during moments of doubt. One of my nurses, Mary Lou, offered me a glimmer of hope. "In two years, Sheryl, you'll be running a marathon, and I'll be there to cheer you on!" Her words planted a seed although I didn't realize it then. Picturing her at the finish line became a source of motivation and a symbol of the resilience I willed myself to achieve, given time and perseverance.

Even though I relied upon nurse Mary Lou's encouraging words, it was incredibly difficult for me to be dependent upon others. I recall feeling helpless and frustrated. In my previous life, I'd prided myself on my independence. Before the burn unit, I was always on the go. When suddenly everything changed, it was like crashing into a brick wall at full speed. I found myself with excessive time on my hands, unable to do even the most basic tasks without assistance. Other people had to do everything for me, according to their timetable, not mine—eating, drinking, going to the bathroom, taking care of dressing changes, and wound care. Letting go of my pride and accepting that I couldn't manage on my own made me feel like a passenger in my own life.

Certain incidents stand out. I recall the time a nursing assistant helped me bring a glass of milk to my mouth. It slipped from my bandaged hands, spilling everywhere. "You have to be more careful!" she said a stern and raised voice, as though I was a child who couldn't manage even the simplest task. Stunned speechless by her harshness, a sense of helplessness washed over me. It was demoralizing.

And there were times when I felt the medical staff treated me as if I couldn't possibly comprehend what was happening around me. Instead of taking the time to explain procedures or to discuss the changes occurring within my body, they simply went about their tasks. This made me feel like a passive recipient of care, rather than an active participant in my own recovery. I had more education and life experiences than some of the staff, but now I was "the patient in bed two" with no identity.

There was a medical resident on the burn unit, Jim, who seemed to recognize and respect my need for human connection. After attending to other patients, he'd come to my room. Our conversations covered global events and our personal interests, our families, and our aspirations. The exchanges provided the intellectual stimulation I missed so much. My mind reawakened, reminding me I held value beyond being "the patient in bed two." I was more than my injuries, and I still possessed my identity, my intellect, and my humanity. These precious visits made me feel like more than a passive figure confined to a hospital bed.

After my donor sites and grafts started to heal, the next surgery loomed. It would involve taking skin from my front upper thighs to cover raw areas on the backs of my shoulders. It seemed like a logical step, but I was apprehensive to undergo another surgery, with good reason as it turned out. When I woke up, I found myself in a horrifying position. Was I hallucinating? My arms were suspended from a rack above my hospital bed, with long, sharp pins penetrating my wrists to keep them in the air.

The purpose of this torturous contortion was to make sure my shoulders didn't touch the bedding, to allow them to heal properly and to prevent the grafts from slipping. My mobility had to be severely restricted to avoid any sudden movements that would compromise the delicate grafts. I couldn't help comparing my situation to the nails through Christ's body during the crucifixion. What a thought. Lying in that posture for several days was excruciating, the ordeal a test of my endurance and mental toughness. I could only pray that being suspended for days with pins penetrating through my wrists, an immense physical and emotional toll, would ensure my grafts would heal. I persevered, hoping to restore my body and to reclaim my life.

Burn unit visitation had to be strictly regulated. Only immediate family members were allowed in during limited times of the day, and unexpected visitors were turned away. Anyone coming onto the burn unit had to wear special protective garments to prevent patients' exposure to germs. That meant long-sleeved gowns, plastic gloves, coverings over their shoes, and shower-cap-style head coverings, with only their faces showing.

One morning, just as the sun was rising, I woke up to find Judge Devitt standing over me. The Chief of the United States District Court for the District of Minnesota, a friend I'd made as a federal prosecutor, stopped to see me on his way to the courthouse. He was violating the visitors' policy by coming so early, but nobody asked him to leave. Looking like central casting for federal judges with white hair, a gentle demeanor, and an angelic smile, he said, "I understand what you're going through, Sheryl. I survived horrific burns during the war when I swam through a sea of burning oil. You're a strong woman. I've seen you in the courtroom and know that you can make it through this." The Judge made regular visits. Not just social calls, but a bridge of shared understanding that connected us in a way that words alone could not convey. His ability to empathize brought me rare comfort during those difficult days.

A former Republic Airlines pilot who'd been a patient in the same burn unit also visited me after the head nurse reached out to him. His appearance was shocking—his right ear half missing, his nose flattened and crooked, his asymmetrical nostrils, his one eye bulging slightly while the other was more sunken—were the result of a harrowing airplane crash that ended his career. Still, I was encouraged to see living proof of the strength that could emerge from adversity. Time and perseverance were allies on my journey to healing. Like Judge Devitt, he was more than just someone passing through my hospital room. Both men were kindred spirits, offering promise of a future beyond the burn unit.

A few days following my second surgery, I was assailed by alarming bloating and a weight gain of over 60 pounds. I perplexed the medical staff as they attempted to identify the underlying cause. Then an overwhelming wave of nausea crashed over me, leaving me gasping for air. The sensation was overpowering, twisting my stomach into knots and causing my body to jerk involuntarily. And without warning, I began to vomit uncontrollably as if my entire body was caught in a violent storm, my muscles convulsing like a ship tossed in a tempest, the retching in waves, relentless and powerful. It left me drained and my body in turmoil.

"I contacted Dr. Solem," the head nurse said with a swift sense of urgency. "We don't want you to get any worse. He's on his way here to see you tonight." It concerned me that my situation might be life-threatening if the surgeon was coming in late on a Sunday evening to see me. I prayed that the doctor's arrival would bring answers and relief before my strength dissolved. What unfolded was unexpected and beyond my worst nightmare.

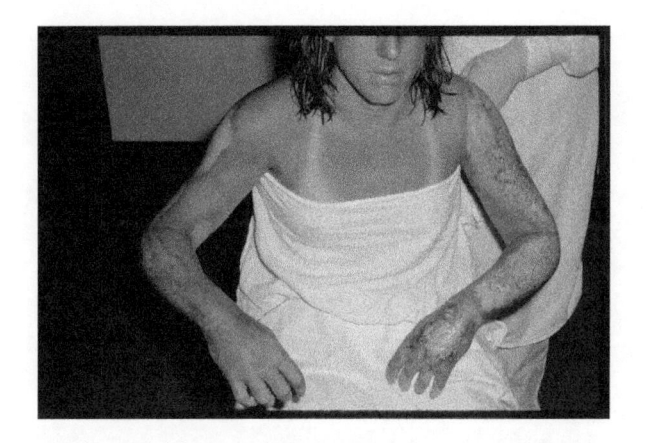

Full body photo showing burns after crash

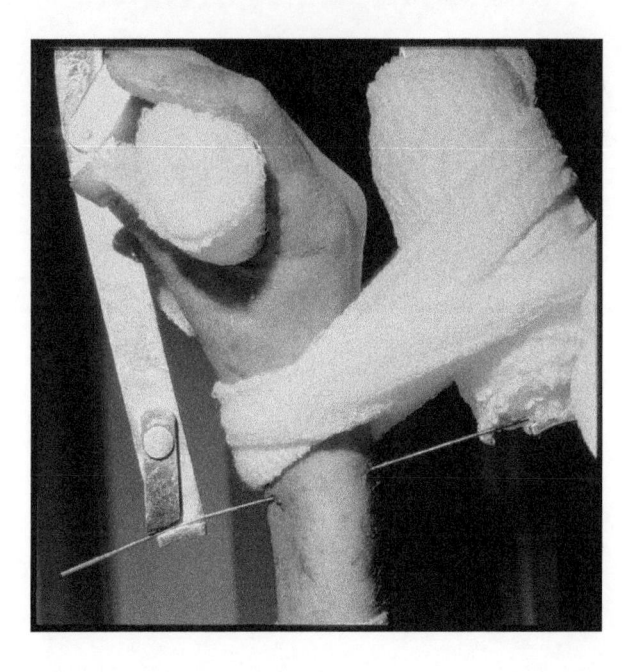

Living Life Full Throttle

My position following shoulder grafts

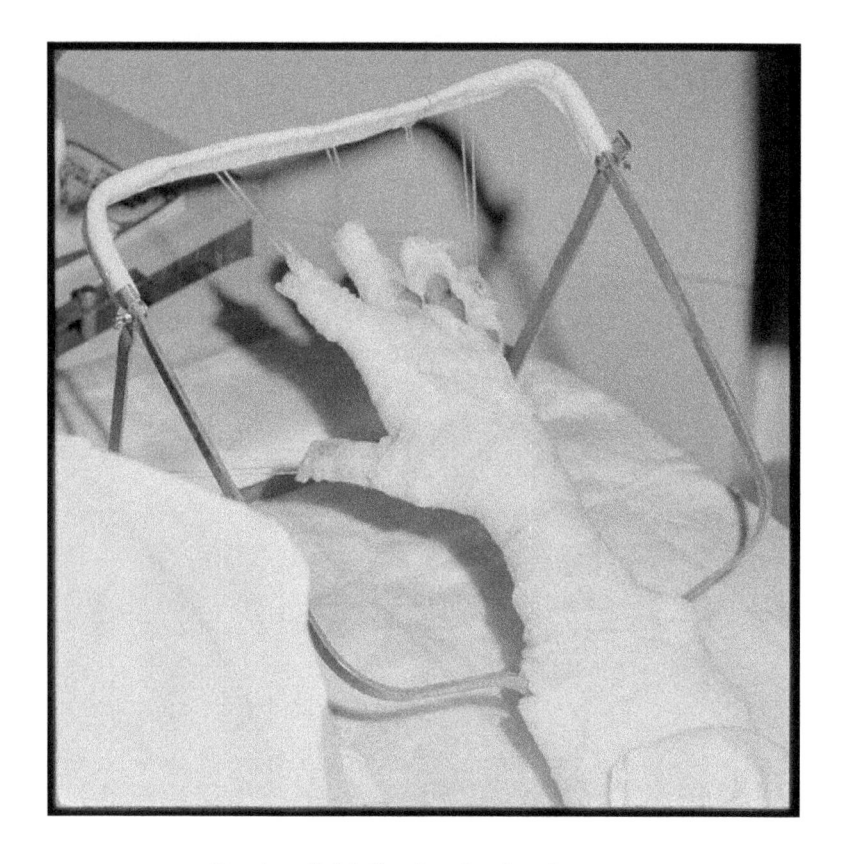

"Banjo split" following first hand surgery

CHAPTER 3

At Death's Door Again

Dr. Solem rushed into my hospital room. His voice shattered the silence like a bullet through a windshield, "Quick, get transport in here NOW. She needs to go down for an X-ray."

Mom pressed cold compresses to my forehead as I writhed in pain. "You'll be okay, honey. They'll find out what's wrong so they can help you," she said. The lack of color in her face belied her comforting words.

My husband leaned down, gently placing his warm lips against my forehead.

"Don't worry, we'll be right here with you." Every cell of me screamed something was seriously wrong.

Almost immediately, the transport team sprang into action.

They swept me off my hospital bed and onto a gurney. An IV bag was hung from a pole attached to the gurney, clear fluid steadily dripping through a thin tube into my arm. Team members, clad in navy scrubs and white sneakers, flanked the gurney, one pushing a portable monitor on a small cart as we sped down the hallway. The monitor beeped rhythmically, displaying my vital signs in bright, fluctuating lines, the gurney's wheels squeaking softly, and doctors and nurses moved aside to let us pass.

When we finally reached the radiology department, the double doors swung open automatically. The room was cool and dimly lit, a contrast with the bright corridors. X-ray technicians moved me onto a cold steel table beneath the large, mechanical arm of the X-ray machine and began taking images. "Take a deep breath and hold it. Don't move," the technician said. I closed my eyes, praying that this procedure would provide answers to the agonizing mystery.

When the X-ray images appeared on the screen, the room seemed to hold its breath. The medical team huddled together, their eyes fixed on the images. Their hushed conversations and somber expressions confirmed this was not a minor issue. I was transported back to my hospital room where the atmosphere was just as thick. My family's concerned faces mirrored the turmoil of emotions within me.

"The X-rays showed free-floating gas in your abdomen," Dr. Solem said. "Air pockets stood out like ominous shadows against the backdrop of your organs. You likely have an ulcer, but we can't afford to speculate." His demeanor was both clinical and compassionate. "It could be a very serious problem. We need to do immediate exploratory surgery to uncover what is wrong."

Could a simple ulcer cause such concern? I thought. What else could it be?

"Get the transport team here right away," he told the nurse. There was no time for questions or going over consent forms.

I found myself on a gurney once again. The transport team worked in a frenzy, their movements swift and intentional. My family's words of reassurance couldn't mask their fright as they kissed me goodbye. Mom's voice broke through the silence, her words like a warm embrace. "Everything will be all right, dear," she said in a quivering voice. "We're saying lots of prayers. God will protect you." I clung to those words like a lifeline, believing that no matter what lay ahead, I was surrounded by love and protected by the watchful eye of a higher power. Even so, my mind raced to understand what was about to take place. What did this mean? Was I going to die?

Like a scene from a medical drama, the operating room, intense with each team member focused on their tasks, they moved me onto the operating table. The bright lights above me were blinding, and the room was cool, filled with the sterile scent of disinfectants. Dr. Solem reviewed the last details with his team, while the anesthesiologist introduced himself with a reassuring smile.

"I'm Dr. Larson. We'll get started now," he said calmly. "I'm going to give you some medication to help you relax." He adjusted the IV line in my arm, and I felt a cool sensation as the medication began to flow. Dr. Larson leaned closer to me, placing a mask over my nose and mouth. "Just breathe normally. You'll start to feel a bit drowsy." I took several breaths before my eyelids grew heavy, and my vision blurred. The soft hum in the room began to fade. "You're doing great. We'll take good care of you," was the last thing I heard Dr. Larson say before I drifted into unconsciousness.

Waking up from the surgery was like slowly emerging from a dense fog. At first, everything around me felt distant, my body heavy and disconnected. Sounds were muffled. Slowly, I began to regain a sense of awareness, and voices began to solidify into words. I blinked hard to clear the haze from my brain, but there was a strange, lingering grogginess that made it hard to grasp where I was or what had happened. I heard my mother saying,

"The surgery is over, dear. You're coming out of the anesthesia."

Dr. Solem began in a matter-of-fact manner, "When we opened you up, a huge amount of air escaped from your abdomen. We'd never seen this before during all our years of treating burns." My mind couldn't grasp what he was saying.

"Your small intestine had burst, letting loose a cascade of infection that invaded your internal organs. The contents of your colon filled your entire body cavity, and the infection spread throughout your stomach, liver, kidneys, spleen, and pelvic organs." The tone of his voice conveyed his concern. "We had to use extraordinary measures to save you."

The condition sounded both foreign and ominous and far more dangerous than an ulcer: peritonitis. "We had to remove 18 inches of your small intestine. The tissue was dead and had lost its viability." The severity of my situation sank in as Dr. Solem revealed the details of the surgery. "For six hours, the team worked to remove each of your organs multiple times, soaking them one by one in saline solution to eliminate every trace of infection. Any remnants left behind could be fatal. We then doused your organs with an antibacterial solution."

There was no sugarcoating the truth. "After repeatedly cleaning your entire body cavity, we had to resort to something drastic: an ileostomy. We created an opening called a stoma through which your intestinal waste can leave your body. It will flow into an external bag attached to your skin that will have to be emptied several times a day." Emptying a bag with my body waste? I grappled with the details of my condition. What was an ileostomy anyway? What did it mean that a bag would be attached to my body? A bag. Would my bowels no longer function?

The doctor's furrowed brow mirrored my own disbelief. He continued, "This condition was likely caused by an anomaly in your intestine. As you lay in the hospital bed after the crash, your intestine folded over on itself, causing it to burst and put your life at risk." Was I at death's door again?

"We faced another critical decision. The incision we made stretches from your breastbone down to your pubic hair. We couldn't sew you up because we might have to go back into the same area. Rather than sewing up your incision, as we ordinarily would do, we put large metal clamps along its entire length, an unconventional but effective way to hold the skin together so that the incision can heal."

The suggestion that I might have to undergo additional surgery alarmed me. And when Dr. Solem said that I'd be "in the woods" for the next two weeks, it spiked my terror. "To combat the infection," he said, "we will infuse your body with an extremely potent antibiotic, leaving no room for the infection to linger and wreak further havoc." I tried to read between the lines. Was there any hope? Little did I know at the time that the odds were stacked against me. I'd been given a slim chance of surviving the peritonitis.

Years later, my surgeon confided that he and his partner had actually given me less than one percent chance of survival. The infection running rampant within me posed a significant threat, and the medical team was doing everything they could to save my life.

The relentless battle raged on day after day. Heavily sedated, I found myself merely an onlooker in my own struggle for survival. My journey was a slow, arduous climb from the depths of despair. Time lost all meaning as my existence hung precariously between life and death. While my family stood vigil by my side, I drifted through the murky water of uncertainty for two excruciating weeks. The future looked bleak.

Gradually, the impenetrable fog of doubt began to lift, and slivers of hope broke through. The powerful antibiotic regimen that had been my lifeline was halted, signaling that the battle was beginning to swing in my favor. I could feel my strength returning bit by bit, igniting a fierce determination within me to reclaim my life from the grip of death.

But it was a tough challenge to adapt to the bag, a device that held a weight of its own in my newly reshaped life. A portion of my small intestine now protruded from my abdomen. An external pouch affixed to my skin, the conduit for digested food and waste to exit my body, needed to be emptied several times a day, a gross departure from the way my body had functioned before the surgery. I had to find a way to come to terms with it.

Dealing with the bag reminded me, in the most humbling way, that I no longer possessed control over the most basic elimination function, which I had previously taken for granted. Every movement, every action was influenced by this new appendage. More than just a physical inconvenience, the bag struck deeply at my self-perception. I felt like a vulnerable infant in need of frequent diaper changes. Stripped of the trappings of adulthood, I'd returned to a state of dependency.

The bag required constant attention and care. Sometimes its contents leaked, soaking through my clothes and releasing a pungent odor that was impossible to ignore. The acidic contents caused a persistent burning sensation on the unhealed donor site to which it was attached. Each change of the bag, each discomforting leak, reminded me that my reality had irrevocably shifted.

The surgeon assured me that the ileostomy was temporary and could be reversed once my intestine healed. However, the uncertainty of when and if that would happen added to my emotional burden. I was anxious, embarrassed, and frustrated. An ever-present reminder of my damaged body, the bag affected how I saw myself.

To help me with the adjustment, my family reached out to a dermatologist who'd treated me for acne during my adolescence. He'd been living with a permanent ileostomy for many years. His support and experience dealing with the bag were invaluable in helping me cope. He recommended I see a stoma therapist who reassured me that my feelings were normal and suggested that I opt for decorative and perfumed bags to hold the contents of my intestinal waste. I was skeptical. How much of a difference could these cosmetic measures make in my overall outlook? I doubted that pretty patterns or pleasant smells could change how I felt about wearing a bag.

These were superficial enhancements. Acceptance and healing for me would require finding inner strength, seeking emotional support, and learning to embrace my new reality.

Days and weeks went by, consumed by many hours of occupational and physical therapy. The therapists began to work on my ability to stand up straight, which had been impeded by the long incision down my middle. They had me walk the burn unit hallways, gripping an overhead bar as I tried to fully extend my arms above my head. This exercise was crucial to ensure that skin on the grafted areas behind my shoulders and beneath my armpits was stretched, so I could regain range of motion and function.

My family knew I was on the mend when my appetite began to resurface. Cravings dominated my thoughts. "I long for the savory taste of popovers from the Flame Room," I told my mother one day. Relieved to see this sign of improvement, she rushed to the Radisson Hotel and returned with them in an hour. Each bite a small victory, life was gradually returning to normal.

Following my abdominal surgery, I had to resume the dreaded tub baths. Pain from the raw areas on my body was excruciating as the nurses lowered me into the tub for each bath, the warm water stinging my tender skin. After each bath, the nurse meticulously applied a topical antimicrobial cream and ace bandages to the areas devoid of skin to prevent infection and aid in healing the severe burns that marred my body, a process requiring patience and precision. Even the slightest mishap would exacerbate my pain. It was a waiting game to see how much of my body would regenerate healthy new skin. Otherwise, additional grafting would be needed. Despite my anguish, I knew I still had to endure these baths that were crucial for my recovery. I remained intent on overcoming the obstacles and emerging stronger on the other side.

The ace bandages encasing my arms and legs acted as a shield, protecting the delicate areas beneath them, but they made me feel like the Pillsbury doughboy—puffed up and overly cushioned. How absurdly bulky I must have looked. Regardless, I clung to the belief that the bandages would eventually be removed, replaced by regenerated skin and restored strength. With my medical team's guidance and my family encouraging me, we pressed on.

Dr. Solem witnessed my progress and perseverance. He made a heartfelt promise. "Sheryl, one day you'll leave the burn unit, and when you do, I will personally escort you out the hospital's front door. No matter what I'm doing or where I am, even if I'm in the middle of surgery, I'll walk out with you. You have my commitment." His words became a powerful source of motivation.

Encouraged by my improving condition, I resumed using the stationary exercise bicycle on the unit. I'd always been committed to exercise. The nurses began to encourage me to envision running a marathon, the goal I'd set for myself prior to the accident. Their faith that I'd improve enough to resume activities that were meaningful to me was inspiring.

I fixated on the expected date of my discharge—August 17th. It was a lifeline that motivated me through the rough times. Despite the doctor's reminder that the original discharge date had been set before my intestine burst, I stubbornly clung to their initial projection.

But another obstacle arose a short while later. Inhaling smoke from the burning cockpit heightened my risk for pneumonia so the medical staff regularly X-rayed my lungs. On a quiet Sunday morning, a resident from the burn team came into my hospital room. He almost nonchalantly said, "Your X-ray has just revealed a spot on your lungs. It looks like pneumonia, Sheryl. So far, you've dodged a bullet, but you may now be meeting your maker."

My mind catapulted to despair. After all I'd been through, all I'd overcome, pneumonia was going to send me to my maker? Before I could formulate any questions, he left me alone to come to grips with this shocking news. My burns had already taken so much from me. Now this hurdle? I sat up in my hospital bed, trying to come to terms with the possibility of mortality at the age of 29, despite my dreams and aspirations yet to be realized. I longed to have a family and to continue my career. My focus was no longer on compiling daily to-do lists; I desperately wanted to live. Had fate chosen a different path for me? I opened my Bible, hoping to find peace.

A few hours later when my mother arrived, I told her the distressing news. Without hesitation, she left my room in search of the burn unit director. She wanted answers, and she wasn't about to rest until she had them. When she returned, she said, "Sheryl, there is no pneumonia in your lungs. The resident was wrong; he didn't know how to read the X-ray. I checked with Dr. Solem, who talked to the radiologist, and he was assured that your lungs are clear." Relief washed over me. A dark cloud lifted, and with a renewed surge of hope I caught a glimpse of the possibility of a brighter future.

Elated by the news, I refocused my attention on my long-awaited discharge date, August 17th, the symbolic milestone in my mind that helped me endure the demands of each passing day. As the time drew nearer though, an uncertainty threatened my already fragile psyche. Whenever I asked the medical team about my discharge date, I'd receive vague and evasive responses. The closer I came to the finish line, the further back it moved, like sand slipping through my fingers. I was consumed by the belief and the promise that my discharge should align with the original timeline. In a maze of uncertainty, I pressed the treatment team for their commitment to a departure from this medical purgatory. Their hesitation was perplexing.

In view of this uncertainty, I embarked on a new mission—to approach each team member individually to plead my case for discharge until I could get everyone on the same page. I presented my arguments to each professional, stressing the significance of having a concrete discharge date for both my family and me. I asked for understanding, saying, "Look at the strides I've made." I tried to assure them I knew that leaving the hospital wouldn't mean my treatments would be over. I expected to continue visiting the outpatient burn clinic for months, possibly even years. Perhaps I could convince them to see the person behind the patient. Eventually, one by one, they came to see it my way.

There was one holdout: Dr. Solem. As burn unit director, his ambivalence was a formidable barrier. He remained noncommittal until shortly before August 17th. Finally, like the breaking of a storm cloud, he, too, relented. But before he would consider it, Dr. Solem set forth some conditions for me. He would allow me to leave only if I returned to the outpatient burn clinic the very next day for dressing changes. He required that I pledge to make regular visits to the burn clinic for aftercare, and to commit to continuing my physical and occupational therapy exercises at home. I was more than willing to pay this price in exchange for my long-awaited liberation.

Looking back, I learned that the road to recovery is rarely a linear trajectory; it's a labyrinth of setbacks and victories, doubt and determination. Moments of uncertainty were equally matched by an unwavering resolve to push through. I began to understand that my voice held power, that advocating for myself was an essential part of the healing process. I also recognized the value of being an active participant in my health journey. At the same time, this experience also taught me the importance of having an advocate like my mother. The day of my discharge was not only a celebration of physical healing, but a victory demonstrating the power of persistence in the face of adversity, the necessity of patience when progress seems slow, and the strength of the human spirit.

As I counted the minutes until I could finally go home, not once did I think of the to-do lists that had been so significant to me before the plane crash. I thought only of how grateful I was for this second chance at life and how I would make the most of it.

CHAPTER 4

Homecoming

Now that Dr. Solem had finally approved my discharge, I could hardly wait. It wasn't just about escaping the hospital. The thought of stepping back into my familiar space, where I could truly unwind and feel at ease, excited me in a way that is hard to put into words.

During my seven weeks in the hospital, I'd been separated from everything that brought me joy. I missed the comfort of my own bed. I could almost feel the softness of the sheets against my skin and the cozy warmth of my favorite blanket wrapped around me—an oasis of comfort after sleeping countless nights in a promise of tranquility—the absence of constant noise, the serenity of an environment untouched by the hustle and bustle of hospital clammer.

I craved being able to read or to just be in the quiet company of my own thoughts. Solitude had always been a source of rejuvenation for me.

As I counted down the minutes until I could finally leave the hospital, never did I think of the once-pressing emails, appointments, and commitments. They'd receded into insignificance compared to the precious blessings of the simple things life had to offer that had taken over my perspective. Gratitude welled up deep within me as I was preparing to return to my familiar sanctuary and a new chapter.

The day finally arrived. Chuck wheeled me down the hallways, and we raced to the exit with my parents at his heels as if we were a gangly band of bandits fleeing with stolen loot. At the doors, he paused and grabbed my sleeve. "Ready?" he said.

"I couldn't be more ready!"

As I made my way out of the hospital doors with Dr. Solem beside me, I was greeted by a sensory feast—nature in all its glory. The vibrant grass, the tranquil sky, the gentle breeze, the songbirds, and the radiant sun—a masterpiece before my eyes. The sheer brilliance of it all, so rich in color, left me awestruck. I recalled the crisp, earthy scent of the grass in my own backyard after a fresh mowing. Above, the sky was adorned with wispy white clouds that resembled the strokes of an artist's brush. Birds singing and chirping created a melodic symphony of breathtaking beauty, an embrace from the world that I had been yearning for. The pain of my injuries and the trauma of the crash were still present, but I vowed that I wouldn't take a moment of this newfound normalcy for granted. Granted a second chance, savoring every day had evolved from a mere notion into a personal mission to live my life fully and intentionally.

But I must have been quite a sight. Wrapped from my neck to my toes in ace bandages covering the burns and donor sites, my wounds were graphic evidence of the trauma I'd endured. I couldn't ignore my anxiety about facing the world with my disfigured body. Myriad questions nagged at me. Would people stare? Would they treat me differently? I wondered how I'd adjust to a world that values appearance so highly. Despite my fears, one thing was clear—I intended to move forward. Ready to rebuild my life, to face whatever was in store, I wasn't about to let this accident define the rest of my life.

Before heading home, we made a detour to the federal courthouse where my dear friend Judge Devitt officed. Working as an Assistant United States Attorney before the crash, I had forged connections with many individuals at the courthouse, but Judge Devitt's friendship held a special place in my heart. I wanted to thank him for his unwavering support and numerous visits while I was hospitalized. He'd been my rock during those long and trying days, a source of comfort in times of uncertainty.

When my parents drove up to the courthouse and pulled into my parking spot, I felt a real sense of connection to the place. I stepped out of our car. Two United States Marshals, who provided security and with whom I'd closely worked, hurried over to welcome me back to where, as a federal prosecutor, I'd tried many criminal cases. Their genuine care and camaraderie showed in their smiles and warm greetings.

The Marshals escorted me inside to see Judge Devitt, whose office was so familiar to me. He approached, with a huge smile on his face, and gently placed his hands on my face. Assessing my condition, he said, "You're fortunate, Sheryl. Your facial burns have all healed." He was right; my face was one of the few visible areas of my body that was not disfigured. His touch and kind words reminded me of his support that had sustained me throughout my recovery.

My voice quivered, "Thank you, Judge, so much, for your visits, your notes, your encouragement. They truly meant the world to me. I don't know how I'd have gotten through these weeks without you."

"It's so good to have you back. Take good care of yourself now. I want to see you in my courtroom again as soon as you are ready." His words deeply touched my heart.

As I stood in Judge Devitt's chambers, it struck me how this journey was not only about healing physical wounds. Rediscovering the strength that comes from genuine connections and the loyal support from friends and colleagues makes the crucial difference in surviving and thriving through times of need. When I left the federal building that day, the courthouse, once a place of work, had now symbolized the enduring bonds that carried me through the darkest of days. I knew that my friends would continue to support me on my journey to becoming whole again.

The next stop was finally home. Snooky, my faithful canine companion for many years, met me at the front door. I'd never seen him leap so high. While he eagerly licked my face, I pulled him close, his short fur prickling the skin under my chin. When my family had brought him to the hospital, he'd stood on a sidewalk five floors below my room, and it may in fact have made me even more lonesome for him. My world had shifted so often, but his unending devotion and affection were genuine.

As I stepped into the house, holding onto my mother's arm for support, a floodgate of emotions overcame me. Our home, filled with reminders of the life I'd been torn away from, things I'd forced out of my mind to survive my time in the hospital, caused tears to stream down my face as the life I'd led before the crash resurfaced. Home was not just a collection of rooms or objects; it was where I felt safety and comfort that had seemed so distant during my hospital stay. With newfound appreciation for the everyday wonders of my home and the life I'd been given a second chance to live, I experienced a homecoming in the truest sense—returning not just to a place, but to the core of my identity.

A wave of exhaustion washed over me, the trip home a mixture of emotions—relief, tension, and lingering pain. The oppressive weight of ace bandages wrapped tightly around my body pinched, making every move a grueling ordeal. They held me together, and yet, paradoxically, caused me to be acutely aware of every inch of my aching body. Each step I took, every attempt I made to find a comfortable sitting position was met with resistance from the tight, constricting embrace of my bandages. Even breathing was an effort. The punishing August sun blazed overhead; the humidity hung in the air, and the thick, sticky air filled my lungs. Simple actions became arduous tasks.

My time at the burn unit was far from over. Following the strict instruction I'd received at my discharge, the very next day I showed up at the burn clinic. I dreaded the thought of returning to the hospital so soon, but I needed to have my bandages changed and to receive additional therapy. Walking back through hospital corridors, apprehension and anticipation swirled in me.

Entering the clinic that morning, I skimmed over the tired faces and anxious expressions in the waiting room. I expected the tedious drudgery of therapy treatments, when my gaze settled on a patient engrossed in the daily newspaper. The bold headline in his hands screamed at me—CRASH! The word halted me midstride. Instantly, my heart started to pound against my chest as though trying to escape the memories. My palms became slick with sweat, the moisture cold and unsettling against my skin. A ringing in my ears, soft at first, quickly amplified to a maddening pitch, drowning out all sounds around me. Trapped in the moment I'd hoped to forget, I gripped the arms of the chair until my knuckles turned white from trying to brace myself.

Time stopped, and the world around me faded to a blur as a vivid flashback unfolded in my mind's eye. I was back there, in my own purgatory. It was futile to remind myself that I was no longer at the crash site, in that chaos. The assault on my senses was relentless. The sharp, acrid smell of gasoline inexplicably filled my nostrils, so real and pungent that I could almost taste it on my tongue. The sound of metal twisting and tearing apart replayed in my mind, and I saw flames consuming everything in my path. The clinic felt like a cage of my own mind's making. I forced myself to move, to seek solitude in a corner of the waiting room. Shaking my head vigorously, I focused on my breathing, on the clinical smells, trying to bring my attention back to here and now.

A short while later, the burn nurse called me into the examination room. My footsteps felt heavy, each step echoing the turmoil that remained. The clinic, where I'd sought healing, had transformed into a battlefield, leaving me to clean up the debris. My heart had not yet settled into its regular rhythm, and my thoughts were a tangled mess. As much as I desired to separate the nightmares of my past from the reality now, distinguishing between the two was tough. The intensity of the flashback began to fade. I wanted to forget it ever happened, but it had left a mark, one that I feared would recur.

I hesitated to share the ordeal with the medical team who were preoccupied with unwrapping my bandages. The examination room, cold and impersonal, felt miles away from the chaotic scene that had played out in my head. My desire to keep my inner turmoil private prevailed. I lay on the examination table under the care team's scrutinizing eyes, bracing myself for the pain that was likely to follow. I forced the terrifying flashback from my mind. Dr. Solem spoke, "Sheryl, your burns and grafts are progressing as well as we can expect. We see no complications." While they cleaned my open incision and packed it with cotton saturated in antiseptic, I asked when—and if—the wound would ever close. The gap down my middle, they assured me, would eventually heal but very slowly and gradually.

After my ordeal at the clinic, I emerged into the daylight. Fresh air caressed my face. I inhaled deeply, attempting to cleanse my mind of the trauma. I resisted recounting the flashback to a professional psychotherapist with every fiber of my being. I wanted to navigate the emotional aftermath of my accident on my own terms, and I believed in my inner strength and resilience now more than ever. Prayer became my refuge as I endeavored to untangle the intricate web of memories and reality.

Initially, my clinic visits consumed several hours every other day. I could not drive, so my mother—who had moved in with us to ease the burden on Chuck and me—dutifully chauffeured me to and from my appointments, a fifty-mile round trip through urban traffic. We all knew the regular check-ups and therapy sessions were key to my rehabilitation.

The occupational and physical therapists continued to focus on my hands, which remained stiff. Bending my fingers was still impossible. Their instructions included exercises I'd already thought I'd mastered such as attempting to clench my fists and to make "tabletops"—bending at the knuckles and extending the fingers as straight as I could. They stressed the need for me to continue reaching overhead as high as I possibly could, grasping door frames to keep the skin on my shoulders and beneath my armpits from atrophying and becoming immovable. The importance of doing my exercises both at home and in the clinic was critical, especially while the burn grafts were still young and before the tissue had a chance to deteriorate. I was a diligent patient, intent on regaining the range of motion and strength I had lost. My progress was painstaking, but I vowed to regain as much function as humanly possible.

The daily routine seemed endless. The graft and donor sites still had countless open sores that demanded meticulous care, which my mother provided. She applied the antiseptic cream gingerly, but it stung as she put it on my wounds. And of course, my ileostomy bag had to be changed, weighing heavily on my spirit like an unshakeable shadow. To say it bothered and embarrassed me to see her handling my bodily waste, much as she did when I was an infant in diapers, is an understatement. These activities consumed hours every morning. The long hospitalization had sapped my stamina and strength. Fatigue invariably set in right after completing the regimen, and I would need to rest.

Although my ileostomy and burns were tough on me, I hadn't predicted that they'd be even more difficult for Chuck. At the time of my accident, we'd been married less than three years. Still in the "honeymoon phase," our physical attraction was strong, our chemistry excellent. My husband rarely touched me after the accident. I tried to give him the benefit of the doubt, thinking that he was being protective, but still his response was difficult to accept. I suspected I was unattractive to him. It diminished my self-image even more than the physical injuries and the bag had already done, and the emotional distance that developed between us became a barrier. At the time, I didn't expect it would continue to build. In hindsight, I should've found the courage to be open about how his behavior was affecting me. Instead, I suffered in silence.

Another situation bothering me since my discharge was the unsettling encounters with strangers. I remember standing in a cafeteria line one day after therapy at the hospital when a stranger stared at my ace bandages. He asked, "Whatever happened to you?" My anxiety surged. I felt frustrated, embarrassed, demeaned, and vulnerable. While I understood when curious children asked, it baffled me that adults felt entitled to pry into my life and condition. I was unsure how to respond. Should I say I was burned in a plane crash? I knew there'd be more questions than I had the energy to answer.

I shared my concern with the doctor who offered a simple, but effective solution. He advised me to reply, "Do I know you?" This seemed to disarm the busy bodies, the prying intruders who said nothing more. The meddlers moved on and gave me back control of these interactions. It may have been a minor victory, but it left me with a sense of empowerment.

Although still in the process of recovering from my burns, I was eager to return to my professional practice. I longed to go back to the trial work I was passionate about. I admit that when I first left the hospital, I vowed to cherish the present in this new chapter of my life. But as my health improved, I encountered an unexpected struggle. This internal conflict surprised me. I missed the identity I'd painstakingly built, and I hadn't anticipated that recovery would also mean grappling with a sense of loss for the person I had been. I broached the subject with my doctor. Dr. Solem emphasized the importance of being patient and of regaining my strength. The healing process would take time. Still, I tried to pin him down on a date when I could return to work. The doctor outlined a plan: in a few weeks' time, he'd allow me to return to my office for two hours a day. After that, I could increase my work an hour each week based upon my stamina and progress. While part of me was eager to dive back into the profession I loved, I recognized Dr. Solem's plan had validity, and I deferred to his recommendation to take things slowly.

My first day back at the United States Attorney's Office three months after my accident was unforgettable.

My parents escorted me through the front doors of the courthouse where we took the elevator to my second-floor office. I hesitated before entering the office. Would my colleagues see me as weak and dependent now that I was all bandaged up and using a walker? It'd been a long journey to reach this point, and the significance of the moment wasn't lost on me. Lois, the front-desk receptionist, must have sensed my trepidation. Her friendly smile and genuine excitement eased my apprehensions. Before I knew it, the entire staff had caught wind of my return, gathering around to greet me. I was returning to a place that held not just professional significance, but also a sense of belonging and connection.

They suggested that I take some time alone to readjust to being back in my office. So thoughtful. The next two hours flew by. Despite my desire to tackle tasks and get updates on my cases, fatigue crept in. My parents reminded me to take it easy, doctor's orders. A twinge of reluctance tugged at my heart. Walking away from an environment that had given me purpose and a sense of identity was bittersweet, but I confess my energy had waned. Interacting with my fellow attorneys had been physically and emotionally draining, so we left for home. It was the sensible thing to do.

Perhaps I was fooling myself. It seemed even to me that I was still holding tightly to my former professional self, still attempting to maintain a grip on the familiar life deeply ingrained in me. Every visit to the burn clinic, I petitioned the medical staff for permission to dive back into full-time work. Every time, they urged me to focus on regaining my strength first. It underscored the reality of my current physical limitations. Each week, they approved spending an extra hour here and there, although the progress felt agonizingly slow. I longed for more, but I walked a tightrope between my eagerness to return to being a trial lawyer and Dr. Solem's efforts to hold me back. Each day, I put in a few hours at the office only after doing outpatient physical and occupational therapy sessions at the hospital first. The remaining hours of my days, if there were any, focused on piecing together the life I'd left behind. Reclaiming it was a constant battle between my determination to go full speed ahead and the limitations of my healing body.

A crucial lesson I learned the hard way was that my burn recovery had only just begun when I was discharged from the hospital. When therapists told me it could take up to two years to regain full use of my hands, I could hardly believe it. But as I slowly regained partial use, I realized that I had to adopt time as my best friend. "No regrets" became my motto as I did all that I could to return to my old self as much as possible. It was a continuing, ongoing journey that rested squarely on my shoulders. From that point on, I had to take ownership, and nobody else was responsible.

Another major concern that weighed heavily on me was having my ileostomy reversed, freeing me from the burden of wearing a bag. Emptying the bag filled with my body's waste products several times daily had become intolerable. The tape that secured the bag to my abdomen was damaging my skin so whenever the bag leaked, the raw skin would sting. I longed to rid myself of it. I begged the burn clinic team for the reversal surgery.

Dr. Solem hesitated. "Sheryl, I worked so hard for many weeks to save your life. Honestly, now that you're back on your feet, the thought of putting you under anesthesia and opening you up again terrifies me." My heart sank. I'd been so focused on the reversal that his apprehension hadn't registered with me. "It's not my area of expertise. You were my first experience with this type of problem. I believe it'd be best for you to see a specialist in gastroenterology to reconnect your small intestine. In any event, it'll likely be a few months before you're ready for surgery."

Thanking Dr. Solem for his honesty and the tremendous effort he had put into saving my life, I assured him I understood his concerns and told him I'd make an appointment at Mayo to see a gastroenterologist. I left the burn clinic with a heavy heart. My path to healing was far from over, but I remained hopeful that one day I would bid farewell to the bag and return to normal.

My clinic visits became a recurring ritual while I navigated the ups and downs of healing. The doctors, nurses, and therapists worked tirelessly taking care of my incision, grafts, and donor sites and improving my movement, strength, and range of motion. About a month after being discharged from the hospital, the open sores on my body had sufficiently healed so I could begin wearing Jobst garments. This closely fitted body suit is prescribed to inhibit the growth of excessive scar tissue and to decrease the severity of scarring by applying even pressure to the grafted and donor sites.

It was a bittersweet transition from ace bandages to Jobst garments. While I was relieved to no longer be wrapped from head to toe in layers of bandages, it was uncomfortable and confining to continuously wear a long-sleeved jacket that zipped up my front, gloves covering all but my fingertips, and leggings that extended over my toes all day and night, except during bathing. In warm weather, the tight-fitting garments didn't breathe well or allow sufficient air flow on the skin, which added to my discomfort. And imagine wearing Jobst leggings over my ileostomy bag. The compression from the leggings caused the bag to dislodge and the seal to break away from my skin, leading to unfortunate leaks obviously oozing through the front of my clothing and emanating a putrid odor.

When I was finally able to spend more time at the office, I looked forward to reentering the courtroom. The memory of my first day back in court will forever be etched in my mind. Judge Devitt was presiding over the corporate tax case I'd been working on at the time of my accident. Several lawyers from New York City law firms along with local attorneys for the corporation were sitting at counsel table for a motion hearing when Judge Devitt entered the courtroom. His law clerk gaveled him in. The judge began by calling the attorneys forward, summoning us to approach the bench where he was sitting. As I came forward, the judge's eyes met mine, and he greeted me with a warm smile.

Judge Devitt gestured toward me in front of the gathered group and shared with everyone that I had narrowly escaped death in a recent plane crash and had just been discharged from the burn unit. He then said, "Sheryl, we are so happy to have you in court for your first appearance since your accident. Welcome back!" I was deeply touched. Judge Devitt recognized the big step it was for me to finally be able to return to court.

A short time later just after Dr. Solem had delivered the news that he feared subjecting me to anesthesia again, I made an appointment with a Mayo Clinic gastroenterologist. I experienced unsettling anxiety at the prospect of undergoing a reversal surgery for my ileostomy. To complicate matters, the flight to Rochester would be my first time on a plane since the crash. Walking up the jetway and boarding the SkyWest regional jet, a second flashback, as vivid and debilitating as the first one three months before, replayed scenes from my crash. My palms became sweaty, and my heart hammered against my chest. The once familiar, now eerie, drone of the jet engines reawakened a deep-seated dread. Breathing in panicky, shallow breaths, I struggled in vain to quell my anxiety. As if the inferno that had once surrounded me was near again, the sharp, bitter smell of fuel filled my nostrils. The pain was palpable. I felt the heat of the flames that had engulfed the cockpit, and the scars that covered my body prickled and resonated with the intense heat from my memory.

I fell into my seat and jerked the seat belt tight. As the engines revved up, that fateful solo flight haunted me—especially the screeching metal, as I fought to escape the wreckage. The memories tried to tug me back to the time of my crash. I couldn't let myself go there. I wanted that ileostomy reversed, and nothing was going to stop me. I said a silent prayer and grasped my mother's arm. In a reassuring voice, she said, "It's a huge step for you to take this flight, Sheryl. In just an hour, we'll arrive in Rochester, where you'll be able to schedule the surgery you want so badly. I'll be right here with you the entire time."

As the plane taxied along the runway, I gripped the armrests until my knuckles turned white. Every shift and shudder of the aircraft caused my body to stiffen in anticipation of a disaster that, logically, I knew was improbable, but my heart feared was imminent. The sensation of lifting off the ground sparked a surge of panic. Mom, sensing my anxiety, reached over to take my hand in hers and said, "We'll be there shortly. Just hold my hand. You're doing great." Despite the uneventful flight and her comforting words, I couldn't shake the sense of looming disaster.

The aircraft maintained its course, and the casual smiles of the flight crew, the relaxed attitude of fellow passengers, and the serene sky visible through the window all indicated that flights don't always end in calamity. When the plane finally landed a little more than an hour after takeoff, my body twitched and tingled uncontrollably from exhaustion. As we walked across the terminal to claim our luggage, I experienced a feeling of achievement. I'd just flown for the first time since the crash. I'd faced my history, and although I'm marked by it, I'm not defeated.

But there was still trepidation ahead. At the Mayo Clinic, I met with the doctor who would perform the reversal surgery. "I'm terrified of this procedure," I said, my voice reflecting the underlying fear that had taken root in my psyche.

He reassured me, "It's a simple procedure; I've done it hundreds of times. What are your concerns?"

"I'm afraid I won't come out of it this time," I said, not mentioning that I'd had a premonition I would die during the operation. The shadow of fear remained with me. It was as if my previous surgery that triggered the need for an ileostomy had formed an indelible link between medical intervention and unwanted results. I tried to reason with myself. *Courage, Sheryl. You no longer have peritonitis. The new surgeon is very capable.* Nevertheless, the mere thought of going under the surgeon's knife once more and the fear that the ileostomy might resist reversal made my blood run cold.

Worry brewed within me as the day of surgery drew near. The night before the surgery, I lay awake, my mind swirling with visions of the austere operating room, the cold steel instruments, and the sensation of being put to sleep again. When I was wheeled into the chilly operating room, gripping the edges of the gurney, a wave of terror washed over me. I took deep breaths, each inhale an attempt to steady my racing heart. But the anxiety persisted, as did the panicky thoughts that fueled it. I couldn't help but remember the unexpected result of my last abdominal surgery—that nasty bag I'd been living with. What if there were complications this time? Was my life once again in danger?

Afterwards, when the haze of anesthesia began to slowly recede, the room gradually came into focus. Blinking against the soft light filtering through the curtains, I became acutely aware of unfamiliar sensations in my body. The rise and fall of my chest felt different, almost as if I were learning to breathe anew. Then a profound sense of relief cascaded over me, soothing the frayed edges of my nerves pulled taut in the days leading up to the surgery. I was alive. I'd made it through the surgery. A voice broke through the stillness. It was the surgeon speaking with assurance that the surgery had gone well. The residual grogginess lifted with a curious mixture of hope, relief, and a thread of uncertainty. The journey, I knew, was not yet over.

The surgeon's measured words seemed to reverberate through my being, adding a new layer of complexity to my whirlwind of emotions. "The success of your surgery is now inextricably linked to an ordinary bodily function—a bowel movement. We cannot be sure that the small intestine is properly functioning until that happens, so we'll just have to wait and see what occurs in the next 24 hours or so." That simple act—having a bowel movement—had been transformed into a pivotal milestone that would dictate the course of my recovery. There was nothing I could do but wait—not my forte.

The ileostomy bag no longer clung to my body. In the quiet hours of recovery, I lay there absorbing the significance, its absence a tangible freedom, a liberation from the physical burden that had been a constant reminder of my struggles. And it was more than just a physical release; it was as if the removal of that bag had also peeled away layers of emotional weight that I hadn't even realized I'd carried. I felt lighter, unburdened from the constraints that had held me captive for so long.

The surgery had been a monumental hurdle, and the surgeon's competence carried me through the ordeal, his skilled hands and comforting words guiding me through my paralyzing fears. Yet, as I gazed toward recovery, my vulnerability was undeniable—the path to healing stretching out like a winding and unpredictable road.

Imagine, waiting for a bowel movement. The hours stretched into what felt like an eternity. Nervous with anticipation, I scrutinized every twinge, analyzed each sensation. The twisting within my stomach, the anticipation and fear danced a delicate duet within me. I lost track of the outside world as my focus waned. Reading a book felt like an exercise in futility, the television screen provided mere background noise, and even the company of visitors was difficult to engage with. The pending outcome held my thoughts captive, leaving little room for anything else.

Then, when the night seemed darkest, the moment arrived. A few hours after midnight, it finally happened: a bowel movement. I let out a joyous shriek that echoed in my quiet hospital room, and the outburst caught the attention of a nurse who came rushing in, concern expressed on her face. She smiled in understanding when I caught my breath and managed to convey the reason behind my exuberance, verifying that I'd successfully passed the long-awaited test. The last remaining obstacle to my discharge now removed, I would finally be discharged.

Sometimes the most mundane events can hold incredible significance, and even the simplest achievements can be cause for celebration. Freed from the constraints of the disgusting ileostomy bag, at long last, I was heading home. Soon I'd be living life full throttle.

CHAPTER 5

Life's A Marathon

It had been a year since Mary Lou, my bedside nurse, asked, "Who's that good looking runner in the photo next to your bed?"

"That was me," I said. "A week ago. As part of my training for a marathon, I ran in a 10-kilometer race sponsored by Bonnie Bell."

"I bet within two years, you'll be running that marathon," she remarked. Mary Lou couldn't have known that her simple words would carry such weight. I was ready to challenge myself. One year after the reversal surgery, I resolved to embark on the daunting task of training for a marathon.

My body was a battleground of wounds. I couldn't even stand up. All my thoughts had to be focused on survival.

But Mary Lou's comment stayed with me throughout my long months of healing, a beacon of hope as I recovered from surgery after surgery. During the year and a half of rehabilitation, I worked tirelessly to regain my strength and mobility and kept the goal of that marathon firmly in mind. As each day brought new hurdles to overcome, I persevered through the bleakest moments of my recovery. I had a singular focus—to make a distant vision of crossing the finish line a reality, despite the fact that I was indeed going through a marathon both literally and metaphorically.

To make training for the marathon endurable and motivating, I reached out to my dear friend, Pat, the news anchor who'd come to the emergency room the night of the crash and had visited me often in the burn unit. Pat had recently quit smoking, and she was looking for a way to maintain her weight. Somehow I convinced her that preparing for a marathon would be an excellent opportunity for both of us to achieve our fitness goals. We recruited two other friends to our team—Sandy and Mary Ann. Pat, ever the journalist, asked if she could document our journey by creating a television story about our small group, which would be training together for our first marathon. We eventually agreed, although initially we were reluctant to train in the public eye.

With this shared goal in mind, we set our sights on running Grandma's Marathon in Duluth, Minnesota, in June of 1981, just under two years after my life-changing accident. Mary Lou's belief that I could run a marathon within two years had stuck with me. Surely a year to get ready for it would be ample time. Now, I was on the cusp of turning that daring aspiration into a reality.

Grandma's Marathon beckoned with beauty and familiarity; the marathon's 26.2-mile route a picturesque journey along the shores of Lake Superior. Chuck and I'd visited the area after my hospital discharge to see the breathtaking transformation of nature's canvas, the fall colors painting the landscape in vivid shades of red, orange, and gold. This stunning scenery would be inspiring during the grueling miles of the race. And so would feeling the cool breeze coming off the lake and the sound of waves lapping against the shores of this natural wonderland. Since Duluth is less than three hours away, our family and friends could easily drive up to cheer us on during the race.

We began training in late summer. My personal goal was simple: I hoped to reach the finish line. Convinced that nearly a year would be more than enough time to accomplish that, I scoured running magazines for recommended training schedules. I gathered information from seasoned runners and fitness experts, and spent hours huddled over my calendar, mapping out each week with ambitious mile targets. I shared the suggested schedule with the others on my team. Our spreadsheets seemed foolproof on paper, and we couldn't help feeling proud of our organizational skills.

At the outset, my muscles, which had languished in idleness for many months, were reluctantly awakened, and they grudgingly resisted any form of motion. On long runs, my legs were unforgiving, often seizing up in painful cramps. Knowing that I had these deficits to overcome, I was intent on improving so that I wouldn't hold the rest of the group back. Although I ran with my partners whenever they gathered, I was willing to go the extra mile to ensure that my training would carry me through the marathon. Adopting the motto, "Do nothing in moderation," I embarked on solo runs, each time going further than before. My goal was to bridge the gap between my current abilities and the level of performance I aspired to achieve.

During my solitary sprints, I was overwhelmingly grateful to be running again, that I'd made incredible physical progress, and even more so, that I recognized the significant shift in my values. Before the accident, I'd been a workaholic, only occasionally seeking the company of others. My days were spent in the office. Taking personal time to go for a long run or to even spend quality time with friends wasn't a priority. Occasionally I'd go for quick workouts, squeezed in here and there at a nearby gym. The crash, my wake-up call, gave me a new appreciation for friends and loved ones whose support had been my lifeline during those long weeks in the hospital. I began to understand how much I'd missed in life while I buried myself in my work.

Fall, winter, and spring passed. We made progress in our training, steadily increasing our endurance and improving our overall fitness levels. It was intense. We'd wake up early in the morning, lace up our running shoes, and hit the pavement. At times, the heavens opened, releasing torrents of rain. We went right through the puddles and trudged through the mud, the drenched clothes clinging to our bodies as symbols of our dedication to the cause. Then came bitter winter days when the world was blanketed in snow, and sleet stung our faces. Although the freezing temperatures numbed our extremities, they couldn't freeze our spirits. The months changed. The sweltering summer heat bore down on us, the bright, relentless sunshine intensifying our struggles and increasing the sweat pouring down our faces. Each season improved our stamina, toughened our muscles, and strengthened our resolve, but didn't upgrade our speed.

At the outset, we stuck to our planned schedule, fueled by the belief that if we followed those meticulous spreadsheets, we'd conquer the marathon. However, our training runs began to take on a life of their own. And then our structured regimen crumbled. Our runs turned into something akin to pit stops for indulgences. Specifically, Dairy Queen breaks. On hot days, we'd find ourselves midway through a long run, drenched in sweat, craving a Blizzard or a sundae. We'd detour from our route to treat ourselves at DQ. Impromptu bathroom stops became another common occurrence. Whether it was poor planning, or urgency brought on by the miles we covered, we often found ourselves searching for the nearest restrooms. These breaks provided opportunities for brief moments of rest, but disrupted our carefully crafted schedules.

To reduce my scarring, I still had to wear the tight-fitting full body suit, which clung to me like sausage casing, resisting every stride. In my compression outfit, I looked like a misplaced astronaut on a mission. The garments acted as an anchor dragging me down because the material didn't breathe. They locked in the heat and created a sauna-like atmosphere. Skin grafts, by the way, do not have sweat glands. The only area that perspired to allow me to cool off was the top of my head. Every step felt like I'd been thrust into a sweltering furnace. To make matters worse, the friction between the unforgiving fabric and my sensitive skin caused raw, tender sores on my body, a test of endurance for my body as well as my willpower. I convinced myself that true strength often emerges from the crucible of discomfort.

Our small training group developed into a source of incredible support. The shared anticipation, dedication, and determination created an atmosphere charged with excitement that knew no bounds. We tackled the endlessly long runs, the demanding speed workouts, and the rigorous endurance-building sessions, logging in hundreds—maybe even thousands—of miles to prepare ourselves for the momentous race. As if our training wasn't enough, we had the unexpected burden of Pat's television crew that followed our every move, our training perfect material for captivating reality TV. They drove alongside us, cameras and microphones in tow.

A fall day stands out. The sun reflected off the glistening surface of the lake as we set off on a routine run. Midway, my feet, which had carried me through countless miles of training, suddenly betrayed me—a perfect storm of clumsiness and bad luck. In the blink of an eye, I stumbled and went down hard. My elbows and knees slammed into the unforgiving pavement, resulting in a trail of blood and the unmistakable sting of embarrassment. Much to my chagrin, the camera crew recorded every moment in all its unfiltered glory. Their lenses zoomed in and filmed me wincing in pain and frustration as I tried to get up from the ground. I unwittingly became the star of our running reality show for all the world to see.

Speaking of feet, I recall another mishap. On a sunny April afternoon training run, the cameraman thought capturing footage of our feet hitting the pavement would be an interesting perspective, a unique angle. He positioned himself prone across the front passenger seat of the car with his colossal and expensive professional camera in hand. While holding the steering wheel in one hand and his camera next to the ground with the other, he leaned out the open door on the driver's side. Anything to get that perfect shot. We continued running. None of us noticed the massive tree looming directly ahead in the car's path. We heard a deafening crash. The impact of the collision not only tore the car door completely off, it sent the cameraman and his precious camera flying. What a sight—the chaos, the screams, and the poor cameraman, nursing his pride as well as his injuries. It was a scene straight out of an action movie.

Our group decided to participate in a series of shorter races to simulate the conditions of a large marathon. These events served as our window into the world of competitive running, offering a glimpse of the bustling crowds, the camaraderie among fellow contestants, and the electrifying atmosphere that accompanied them. We started with modest races—five or ten kilometers. During these races, as I lined up with other runners at the starting line, I could feel my adrenaline surge, and the cheers of spectators filled the air. After completing four training races, our confidence grew. We decided to take on a more ambitious goal: the Syttende Mai run in Grantsburg, Wisconsin, a prestigious seventeen-mile race in celebration of Norwegian Independence Day on the 17th of May. This annual spring ritual was reputed to be "hard to get into." That didn't stop us. Our running group included Pat, the popular Twin Cities Channel 4 newscaster. The race director knew Pat from her years anchoring the news and quickly signed up our team, assigning her race number "4".

We approached the event as if it were a marathon, even though it spared us those final nine miles of Grandma's. The day was cool and slightly overcast, perfect for a race. Just as the horn signaled the start of the race, Channel 4 television station's helicopter flew overhead to film the event. Even if we'd wanted to remain anonymous, it would have been impossible, as the roaring propellers alerted everyone that our team was in the race. The helicopter followed us a good distance, adding an unexpected level of attention to us.

The first few miles flew by. I settled into my pace, finding a comfortable rhythm while navigating through the crowds. The course became more difficult at the midway point, the rolling hills never-ending. My legs grew heavy, and my energy level waned. Doubts crept into my mind, but then I remembered Grandma's Marathon was merely a month away. I ignored my discomfort, drawing inspiration from the fellow runners around me.

Meanwhile Pat had an ongoing feud with her running shoes. A foot doctor had recently prescribed a $200 pair of orthotics for her shoes. Pat took her shoes off to give her feet a momentary respite, but then, without fail, she put them back on and attempted to keep running, repeating the cycle for several miles. I must admit that her frequent stops in the middle of the race trail frustrated me. "Come on, Pat," I urged, irritation evident in my voice. "Just take the orthotics out if they're bothering you. The race will be over, and we'll still be out here on the course." Other runners steadily pulled ahead of us while the delays caused us to fall way behind. Around mile twelve, Pat finally took the orthotics out of her shoes for good and flung them as far as she could. They landed deep in a nearby cornfield, and finally liberated, she put her shoes back on and picked up her pace.

We persevered through the miles that seemed to stretch on forever, refusing to give up and giving it our all. Exhaustion weighed heavily on our bodies, but we finally caught sight of the finish line. I was right: the race had already ended. Alone and trailing behind thousands of other runners, we were dead last. Even the helicopter had given up on us.

No one witnessed our finish. Still, I felt an indescribable mix of exhaustion, elation, and pride. Our performance may not have been noteworthy, but the experience taught me that even when things don't go as planned, it's essential to keep going, to finish what was started. I'd pushed myself to the limit and conquered the physical and mental hurdles along the way. The race reinforced the lessons I'd learned in the burn unit nearly two years before—the importance of perseverance and mental fortitude to get through the tough times. With just a month to go until Grandma's Marathon, I knew I'd need to continue pushing my limits to realize my goal of completing that race.

The day of Grandma's Marathon approached. I was a bundle of nerves and excitement. The hard work and countless hours of training had led to this pivotal moment and had given me confidence that I'd done everything within my power to succeed. Regardless of the outcome, I had no regrets. On the morning of Grandma's, I woke up before the sun and ate a hearty breakfast, making sure to fuel my body well for the demanding physical exertion ahead. Although it's called the "Duluth Marathon," it begins twenty-six miles away in the city of Two Harbors, concluding in Duluth. Runners are not allowed to drive to the start. My teammates and I boarded a bus to Two Harbors, arriving more than an hour before the race would start, and when we walked the one-third of a mile distance from the bus to the starting line, we were surrounded by a sea of fellow runners.

The chill of the morning seeped into our bones. I donned a black garbage bag over my running shorts and body suit to shield myself from the biting cold. It wasn't the most glamorous look, but it kept me warm. Before the race began, I made sure to use the portapotties nearby. When the starting signal rang through the air, we were off.

My partners and I agreed that we would each run our own race, to allow us to focus on achieving our own personal best times without worrying about our running teammates. Running Grandma's, it was just me, the course ahead, and my thoughts occupying me on the journey.

From my very first step, I gained momentum due to the energy of the crowd. The long, expansive route that hugged the breathtaking shores of Lake Superior stretched out ahead, as did the cheering crowds, aid stations, and live bands. The atmosphere was electric, alive with enthusiastic spectators shouting "you can do it" and "looking good, number 2563" from the sidelines along the route. The crowds' infectious enthusiasm spurred me on, and I consciously pushed myself further and faster while I battled the biting cold. The aid stations offered Powerade and water, but I was afraid that if I stopped, I might not get started again. The *Rocky* song blared loudly. It was as if the whole world had come together to support us.

Midway through the race, my initial vigor began to wane, gradually giving way to fatigue that threatened to undermine my resolve. My legs felt like lead, and my mind played tricks on me. Could I finish the race? Although a gorgeous setting, the shores of Lake Superior seemed interminably long. How much further *is* this race? I tried to focus on taking one step at a time visualizing the finish line, and then I shifted my focus to the runners ahead of me, catching up with them one by one as I pressed on. Despite the doubts in my mind, I knew there was no other option for me. Running this marathon meant too much.

With my muscle memory kicking in from the countless training runs I'd endured over the past year, I kept going, consciously purging negative thoughts from my mind. Although I was almost overcome by exhaustion, it couldn't extinguish the fire that burned within me, the rhythm of my footfalls a reminder that I was in control of my destiny. With each step, I repeated to myself, "I won't give up. I will not quit." The run was about proving something, about stretching my limits—limits I'd set for myself, and limits life had set for me.

Although I tended to be a stoic Scandinavian, my heart pounded with sheer joy as I choked back my tears of happiness when I crossed the finish line in 3 hours and 52 minutes. I'd just surpassed the physical and emotional barriers that had once seemed insurmountable. The months of training paid off. I gave it my all, leaving nothing on the course.

Afterwards my running partners and I made our way to a restaurant, where equally elated family and friends—and the camera crew, of course—awaited our arrival. We celebrated our feat with toasts to one another and toy trophies that we awarded to each team member. The atmosphere was vibrant and joyful. We clinked our glasses, raising them high to toast our success, which the television crew filmed. Each of us expressed that the race wasn't about how we'd finished; it was about the journey that had led us there. The countless hours of training, the sacrifices made, and through it all supporting one another had culminated in this celebratory evening. We came to be teammates, competitors, and a tight knit family bound together by our shared pursuit, the true victory not measured by our times but in the memories we'd created and the personal growth we'd experienced. The toy trophies were symbols of our resilience, unity, and the unforgettable journey we'd taken together.

After my running companions crossed the finish line at Grandma's Marathon, they'd had their fill of long-distance running. For me, the marathon became my way of reclaiming my identity and declaring to the world that I was back. I didn't want anyone's pity, and I certainly didn't want people to fixate on the fateful crash anymore. It was behind me, a painful chapter in my life that I was determined to put in the rearview mirror. Pat's television series about our marathon, broadcast statewide, played a significant role in reshaping the narrative about me. It was a powerful shift that allowed me to finally be seen by others and to see myself for who I truly was—not just a survivor, but a fighter, an achiever, someone with dreams and ambitions for the future that no plane crash could take away.

With Grandma's Marathon now in the past, I looked ahead—to set new goals. I wanted to run the Twin Cities Marathon, reputed to be the most beautiful urban marathon in the country, and it was literally in my own backyard. The course wound its way around picturesque Minneapolis lakes, through residential Twin Cities' neighborhoods, and even past the Minnesota Governor's Residence, ending triumphantly at the majestic State Capitol building. And the race would take place in October, when leaves painted the landscape with a breathtaking array of colors.

Unlike my previous attempts with running buddies, this time I'd tackle the training on my own. No ice cream cones and leisurely breaks for me. I aimed to avoid any unnecessary indulgences or time spent idly strolling the trails. I focused exclusively on efficiency and pain management. To prepare for this next challenge, I stuck to my trusted training regimen, diligently logging miles and setting new goals.

The first year of marathon training, a long-sleeved compression jacket concealed my burned arms. I needed to stick to wearing it as well as the full body suit my doctor had prescribed to aid in the healing process. But as time passed, my desire to wear short-sleeved shirts during training runs grew stronger. The prospect of being cooler and more comfortable while running was enticing. When my doctor told me that I no longer needed to wear the jacket, my husband made a comment that shook me. "You should stick with long sleeves. It's more respectful to other people. Baring your scars is hard for others to see." His words hit me like a bucket of icy water. I was torn between my desire for comfort and the fear of judgment. Somehow, my choice of clothing had become a question of respect. I capitulated and kept my arms covered, wearing long-sleeved shirts whenever I ran.

I spent a lot of time alone with my thoughts during my runs, the miles stretching out before me. The rhythm of my footsteps, the sound of my own breathing, and the gentle cadence of nature became my constant companions. I found peace in the simplicity of each stride, appreciating the beauty of my surroundings. It was a personal voyage of self-discovery, testing my physical limits while cultivating mental resilience. And it provided me with the unique opportunity to reflect on the blessings of being alive. If I felt isolated or lonely, I relied upon my inner voice assuring me I was on the right path, urging me to keep moving forward. Fellow runners and I would exchange brief nods or friendly greetings, silently acknowledging our shared passion as we passed each other. These fleeting connections reminded me that even in solitude, I was part of a larger community of individuals chasing their dreams.

The Twin Cities Marathon date was around the corner. I couldn't help but feel a surge of excitement. With each training run, I visualized the vibrant autumn scenery, imagined the roar of the crowds, and anticipated the friendly competition. Because of its urban setting, the cheering crowds would line the streets, far surpassing those at Grandma's Marathon. And the aid stations, sponsored by various civic organizations and businesses, competed against each other to see who could provide the most enthusiastic supporters and fortifying refreshments along the way. It was like a marathon within a marathon—the volunteers' energy rivaling that of the runners.

Running the Twin Cities Marathon would be much easier than Grandma's, especially after completing a previous marathon. It helped that it was a more familiar route, one that I had trained on, and relatively flat. There'd be friends and family along the race course to support me. My self-confidence boosted, I began focusing on my personal best to see if I could improve my time over my run at Grandma's. When the day came, spectators along the way cheered me on by name, not just by number. Overcoming one hill just before the end, I crossed the finish line in 3 hours and 49 minutes—an indescribable moment of triumph. I beat my Grandma's time by three minutes, setting a personal record, and, more importantly, proving to myself that I could survive and thrive.

Twin Cities now behind me, why not take on the iconic New York City Marathon, known for its massive turnout of thousands of runners from all corners of the globe? The annual race traversed the five boroughs of New York City, making it truly an extraordinary experience. With over 50,000 runners and an applicant pool twice that size, it held the distinction of being the largest marathon in the world. The popularity of the event made gaining entry as arduous as the race itself. A few of my work colleagues and I submitted our applications, hoping that we would win the marathon lottery. After receiving news that we were "in," we began our intensive training program spanning several weeks, committed to making the most of this remarkable opportunity.

Bob, one of my training partners for the New York City Marathon, insisted I wear short sleeves while running with him. "You're sweltering in those long-sleeved shirts. You're entitled to be comfortable. Think of your scars as badges of courage," he said. His nurturing support resonated deeply within me, reframing how I saw myself. It took time, but eventually I wore short sleeves on my runs, not just for physical comfort, but also as a declaration—a huge milestone for me. Bob's acceptance, as well as my own acknowledgement that my scars were evidence of battles I'd fought and won. They were to be celebrated rather than hidden. With that realization, I became more comfortable than ever in my own skin.

Finally, the day of the marathon arrived. The atmosphere was electric, as marathoners from around the world gathered at the starting line. The international spirit of the event struck me. The mayor of Amsterdam attended, and he greeted all the Dutch participants. Italians formed an eye-catching display; donning green, white, and red, they ran in the formation of their country's flag. Every imaginable language could be heard among nearly two million spectators, creating a cacophony of excitement. The race commenced on Staten Island near the majestic Verrazano-Narrows Bridge, closed for the marathon. Runners spread out across both sides of the bridge's upper level and the westbound side of the lower level. It was a mesmerizing spectacle.

True to its promise, the marathon took us on a captivating journey through all five boroughs of New York City, featuring areas that we'd otherwise never have ventured into during daylight hours. The course meandered through Brooklyn, Queens, and into Manhattan, providing us with glimpses of the diverse neighborhoods. A tough moment came at the 16-mile mark—ascending the Queensboro Bridge into Manhattan. The steep quarter-mile climb with an average four percent incline tested my endurance. I was dead set on conquering it, but I didn't realize the toughest mile for me was ahead.

The cheering crowds fueling my energy level, the New York City Marathon was quite a leap beyond my comfort zone. Venturing into unfamiliar terrain and navigating the entire route in solitude was different from either of my previous marathons. New York's race had ten times more runners than the Twin Cities Marathon so the course was considerably more crowded. I became distressed. My accident had left me with a severe case of claustrophobia in any situation that mimicked enclosed spaces or confinement. Sure enough, as the marathon progressed, the sheer density of runners on the course triggered a flashback. I was thrust into the burning cockpit, desperately seeking an escape to survive.

By the time I reached mile 17, panic surged through me. My breathing turned shallow and rapid, resisting my every attempt to draw in air. The sound of the plane's engine sputtering and then suddenly stopping reverberated in my consciousness. I couldn't shake how isolated and alone I'd felt then, just as I did now amidst the throng of marathoners. I had to get out of the race. Stumbling onto a bus, I escaped the chaos of the crowds and made my way back to the Central Park finish line, the medical tent, and safety. Once inside the tent, I was promptly given oxygen, orange slices, and a warm blanket to drape over my shoulders. As the fog of panic and exhaustion began to lift from my mind, the realization hit me that despite the progress I'd made since the plane crash, vestiges of the damage remained.

I was devastated that I had to abandon my goal of completing the New York City Marathon. All that work to train for and enter the race was for nothing. My body and spirit though had given me a sign. Leaving the racecourse made me feel liberated. I realized that I didn't need to prove anything to anybody—and most importantly, to myself. What mattered most was that honoring my body was as significant to my self-worth as stepping over the finish line would have been. I felt at peace, and content that my decision to leave the race was the right one for me.

The New York City Marathon would be the end of my marathon-running days and would also mark the beginning of a new chapter in my life. Walking away from the racecourse, I knew I was finally on the path to healing. I'd found something much more valuable—a profound sense of freedom and empowerment, understanding I was in control of my own narrative and my story of triumph over adversity.

I discovered there were many parallels between training for those races and recuperating from my burns. Both turned out to be far more demanding and time-consuming than I'd anticipated. I found myself pushing past my limits and discovering new depths of resilience. Both journeys required single-minded commitment to meticulously crafted schedules that spanned several months. Each day was a small step, a brick laid in the foundation of recovery or race preparation. There was no shortcut, only a relentless pursuit to finish the task, and uncertainty about the outcome. Doubts during my marathon training reminded me of times in my burn recovery when hope eluded me. All I could rely upon was my faith and the support of those who understood the journey. Despite sometimes feeling isolated, as if nobody could comprehend my struggle, I counted my blessings. I was alive, and I'd learned to rely upon that inner voice that assured me I was on the right path, urging me to keep moving forward. In the end, both my training and my burn recovery taught me the importance of perseverance, self-belief, letting go of outcomes, and trusting God.

Finishing Grandma's Marathon

CHAPTER 6
Valuing Family

Before the accident, my husband, Chuck, and I had eagerly planned to start our family. We'd been married almost three years, and at age 29, we felt ready to embrace parenthood with open arms. The plane crash shattered our dreams and put our plans on an indefinite hold. Intimacy, once effortless and joyous, became a maze of hurdles.

At first, the shock of my physical scars was overwhelming. When I looked in the mirror, I could hardly recognize the person staring back at me. The disfigurement from the burns was catastrophic, not just for me but for my intimate relationship as well. Although the bag was gone, my body still bore oozing sores.

An open incision traversed my abdomen from my breastbone to my pubic hair, creating a gap that leaked body fluid.

My scars and wounds necessitated gentleness and sensitivity, and in bed, I wore a hand splint wrapped in ace bandages. One night, Chuck leaped out of bed from a deep slumber and swatted at it, mistaking it for a bat in the room.

Even though the physical aspects were daunting, the emotional hurdles proved even more formidable. I no longer felt desirable, sexy, or confident. I felt guilty about not wanting to be seen. Not by anyone, and especially not my husband. Chuck hadn't signed up for this. When he chose me, I looked different. I wondered if he missed the old me as much as I did, but I knew he must have from the pain in his eyes when he looked at me. The caresses we'd once shared morphed into cautious, apprehensive moments. Every time we got close to each other, I couldn't help thinking about my changed appearance. The scars had etched themselves onto my soul, casting a long, dark shadow on my self-worth.

The challenges seemed insurmountable. Rekindling our sexual connection wasn't something we could achieve overnight, but each time we tried, we encountered new obstacles. I didn't want to let the accident dictate my life and came to believe that if it was God's intention to prevent me from conceiving naturally, we'd have to find other ways. We both shared a deep desire to have a family, and nothing was going to stand in our way.

Our sexual limitations continued in the months that followed. We began to discuss another way of parenting—

adoption. It wasn't a new concept for me. During my childhood, I'd fervently yearned for a sister and had pleaded with my parents to adopt a child. My appeals fell on deaf ears. Our family remained a nuclear unit consisting of my older brother and me. It never made sense to me why they wouldn't adopt, especially given all the love we had to share. While I was growing up, my mother's cousin adopted four wonderful children, who spent a significant amount of time with our family. Their presence served as a constant reminder that adoption was a beautiful and meaningful way to build a family. Then, I didn't know my own journey would eventually lead me to contemplate that very path.

But it took time. After the accident, I'd been thrust into a world of constant adjustments, learning to live with visible scars and to cope with my own disabilities. For two long years, each day began with a trip to the occupational therapist, where I painstakingly struggled through exhausting sessions to regain the use of my hands. I worked to restore my posture by clutching an overhead bar, and I practiced walking. My body, wrapped in ace bandages, often stopped people in their tracks. Their stares, a blend of curiosity and pity, forced me to repeatedly narrate the tale behind my injuries. The grafts I had made me look like a patchwork quilt.

When I could shift my focus beyond my own medical needs, we took the first step. After attending informational meetings at the two largest adoption agencies in Minnesota, in 1980, we submitted our applications to adopt an infant.

During our adoption quest, I was adamant about being genuine with our social workers. This wasn't just about us—it was about ensuring we were the right parents for a child. I chose to focus on what I could do, not what I couldn't, but still I worried about whether I could be the parent that I wanted to be—one my child deserved. And there were my own issues to contend with. Since being trapped inside the burning cockpit, I couldn't be in the same room with a candle. How would I celebrate my child's birthday without candles to blow out on a cake? I couldn't stand up straight due to the incision down my middle, so how would I hold a baby in my arms? The knuckles on my hand wouldn't bend. How would I be able to hold a baby's bottle?

A month and a half after we'd completed our adoption paperwork, I was elated when I received a call from one of the agencies to which we'd applied. The assistant to the social worker assigned to our case asked about scheduling a meeting to discuss our desire to adopt. We set up an appointment for the following Friday morning. When we sat down for breakfast the morning of our interview, I confided in Chuck, "I'm nervous about this meeting. What if the social worker doesn't think we can provide a healthy environment for a child? What do I say when she asks if I'm healed enough from the crash to parent a child?"

Chuck reassured me. "We just need to be honest. She'll see that we are willing to learn and ready to move ahead with our lives. There's no need to be anyone other than who we are. Do you feel ready to be a parent?"

"I think I am," I said. "I want to be a mother more than anything else in the world."

When we arrived at the agency, I felt my heart thudding in my chest and grabbed the rail to steady myself. "I can do this," I mumbled to no one in particular. "Of course I can." But I wasn't entirely convinced. The social worker came out to greet us, her smile warm, yet professional. We exchanged pleasantries before going into her office—a comfortable space filled with books and toys, likely used to make children and prospective parents feel at ease.

There was a heavy silence as we settled into chairs opposite her desk before she looked directly at us both with a measured gaze and asked, "Why do you want to adopt a baby?"

I hesitated. "Well, my husband and I have given this a lot of thought," I said. "I was badly burned in an airplane crash a year ago and have had several surgeries, but now that I am healing—both physically and emotionally—we feel that we are ready to start our family."

She jotted down some notes and then looked up again. With a fixed and concerned look she posed her next question. "Will you need any more operations?"

I nodded. "Just one for certain, a z-plasty to break up the scar tissue between my thumb and index finger on my right hand. It's an out-patient procedure to loosen the skin tightness and will require some occupational therapy after the incision heals." I could see in her eyes she was thinking about the implications of what I said.

"Have you considered how this surgery will affect your ability to care for a baby?"

"Yes," I said. "We've discussed it. Our family will step in to assist with the baby's daily care for the week or so that I'll be unable to use my hand."

Chuck touched my shoulder. "And I'm willing to do whatever needs to be done to care for our daughter while Sheryl's hand is healing." His words were firm, his commitment clear.

"Could you support a child with physical or mental disabilities?" the social worker asked.

"I'm not sure," I said, knowing that I needed to be honest, both with myself and with her. "I'm still a little fragile."

She nodded. "What is the lasting impact of your trauma?"

My voice trembled, but I tried to be strong and clear. "My accident affected me physically, mentally, and spiritually.

The scars on my body from the burns and grafts are permanent reminders of my plane crash. But I've remained sharp and focused, as alert as I've always been. And my spirit? It's only grown stronger. I'm more determined than ever to cherish each day, to live a life free of regrets." I straightened up in the chair and smiled at the social worker. This is going well I thought, that is, until the next question she asked me.

"How will the accident impact your ability to parent?" There it was. The question I'd wrestled with and deep down hoped to avoid. The room felt smaller, the air heavier, as if the space between the walls was charged with the seriousness of the question. I asked God to guide my words. Until then, my fear had been leading, not my heart. Somehow a deep calm settled in me. I knew I was as ready as anyone to love and guide a child.

"Surviving the crash reminded me of life's uncertainty, that tomorrow isn't guaranteed for any of us. I've worked hard to heal from the accident, and I'm committed to embracing life to its fullest. I will be the kind of parent I've always aspired to be."

She held my gaze for a moment, then she smiled.

In hindsight, the interview helped me. I realized love is not the only prerequisite for parenting—resilience, seeking resources, and the readiness to face any obstacles head-on are also essential. After the crash I'd come to believe that my survival was not just a fluke; it must be a sign that there was a purpose, a reason why I'd been given a second chance. I believed I had a duty to make the most out of the life I'd fought so hard to keep. Starting a family had always been a cherished dream, and I refused to let the airplane crash hinder that dream.

When the social worker asked whether we'd be open to cross-cultural adoption, we had no hesitation. "Yes, of course. We'd love to adopt a baby from Korea." Minnesota had the largest population of Korean-born adoptees in the country, and we knew many families who'd adopted from there.

"Korean baby boys are rarely available for adoption because they are highly valued in Korean culture, whereas girls, especially if born out of wedlock, struggle to find their place in society," she explained.

"We'd be thrilled to have a baby girl from Korea," I said. Chuck nodded his agreement.

Later, we discovered there was one person in our family who had an issue with adopting from another country. My father. "Couldn't you find a Caucasian child to adopt?" he asked over Christmas dinner. His question shocked and saddened me. I hadn't anticipated any resistance from him. He'd played such an important role in my recovery, traveling hundreds of miles to be there for each surgery and for my discharge. A man of few words, Dad had always supported the decisions I made. He was typically easygoing. I couldn't have imagined him making that comment. In his defense, I reminded myself that he'd grown up on a farm in a rural state where there was little diversity. His friends and family all had backgrounds like his own. Moreover, he'd also lived through the Korean War. I tried hard to see things through his lens and to focus on helping him adjust. It wasn't a lengthy conversation. I think he understood that I needed his support and so I said, "Dad, please trust me. It's important that you understand our decision and will accept our daughter." After considering his perspective, I still felt strongly we were doing the right thing. His skepticism wouldn't deter us.

After our meeting with the social worker, while we waited for our referral, we decorated the nursery, supplying it with tiny clothes and accessories. I'd never spent much time around infants and toddlers. Growing up, I didn't babysit because my days were always filled with school and various extracurricular activities. As the youngest in my family with no cousins around, I didn't play with or watch any babies or little children. Chuck and I felt it was important to attend parenting classes at the adoption agency to learn about newborns—everything from feeding to diapering, to sleeping and bathing. I knew I was in for a steep learning curve.

We deeply wanted children. At the same time, we recognized how my recovery from the massive emotional and physical trauma was a work in progress. I hoped I'd be able to muster the energy to keep up with a child. Not knowing whether I might need any future medical procedures, I wondered if I was equipped to take this big step. Somehow I knew in my heart that I had the capacity to be a loving and dedicated mother. By the grace of God, coupled with the exceptional skills of medical professionals, I had a second chance to live out the dreams the accident had nearly snatched away. Fear should not dictate my future. I made a solemn pledge that I'd pour my love, care, and attention into my parenting role, come what may. But I had yet another major and unexpected adjustment I would need to make.

When we might receive a referral for an infant from the adoption agency was uncertain. We'd been told the call that a baby had been matched with us could take as long as two years. I tried to mentally and emotionally prepare myself for such a long wait. In the space between now and that elusive future, I was still grappling with the aftermath of the crash. I couldn't quite shake a sense of urgency—a sense that life was fragile, fleeting, and if I didn't do everything now, I might not get another chance. Ironically, just as we were settling into a waiting game, a new judicial vacancy on the Hennepin County trial court in Minneapolis was announced. I didn't hesitate. Besides, the timing of our adoption referral was unpredictable. The call could come at any moment or might not come for years, I reasoned. I felt compelled to apply. The adoption referral felt daunting, but letting the judicial opportunity go would be disheartening. Galvanized to live fully, to take action now, I couldn't let this moment slip by.

Furthermore, the accident altered my outlook in unexpected ways. Before the plane crash, I thrived on the adversarial environment of the courtroom. Constantly getting ready to go to battle, my days were filled with arguing against opposing counsel, presenting cases before judges and juries, and navigating the intricacies of the legal system. The competitive edge that had defined me for so long began to feel out of place. I wished for better balance in my life, no longer finding satisfaction in the contentious courtroom battles. I felt my legal skills could be more constructive and meaningful. In pursuit of my goal to foster healing and unity rather than to perpetuate division, I applied for the judgeship.

A merit selection commission screened dozens of applicants for the position. I was thrilled when they selected me as one of three finalists. The last step in the process involved an interview with Minnesota's Governor Al Quie. My future hinged on my performance. No pressure. I'd prepared extensively, and I thought I was ready to answer questions about my professional background, but the thought of Governor Quie lobbing a curve ball filled my mind with doubts and fears. I arrived at the State Capitol thirty minutes early. After the wait, which seemed like an eternity, the receptionist escorted me into the Governor's office. An imposing man emerged. More than six feet tall with huge hands and a firm handshake, he bid me to sit down facing his expansive oak desk. He had a surprisingly gentle voice. "To begin with, I'd like to hear how you see the differences between justice and mercy."

He caught me off guard. Although I was aware of his deep faith, I hadn't anticipated questions about Biblical principles. I paused. Reflecting on the spiritual teachings I'd studied, I answered with conviction, "Justice, in my view, is about people receiving what they deserve based upon their actions and the law."

"Interesting. And your thoughts on mercy?"

"Mercy, I think, involves compassion and grace, often going beyond the strict letter of the law. It's more subjective and considers the unique circumstances behind each case."

The Governor jotted a quick note in a folder on his desk. "What role do these concepts play in the work of a judge? How would you balance the two?"

"I believe a judge should administer both. Justice is essential for maintaining order and upholding the law, while mercy recognizes how every case involves unique situations. The two—justice and mercy—should be balanced to ensure that the legal system is both fair and compassionate." Governor Quie cleared his throat and then smiled at me.

"Please tell me about yourself."

I clasped my hands together to keep them from fidgeting. After describing my career as a litigator, I wasn't sure how much to reveal about my accident. Would my injuries give Governor Quie pause about my ability to take on judicial responsibilities? Either way, I decided, I should be truthful with him.

"Governor, in 1979, I spent several weeks in a burn unit after surviving an airplane crash. It was a jolt that compelled me to reexamine my career and aspirations, and I became disillusioned with the adversarial nature of litigation. Instead, I'd like my work to align with my personal values, to dedicate myself to seeking the truth. For me, it's not about winning arguments, but upholding justice with an eye toward fairness."

My views apparently resonated with the Governor. His call several days later informed me he was appointing me to the trial bench in Minneapolis. At the age of 32, I was the youngest person in history to be appointed to the position in Minnesota. On October 1, 1982, my friend Judge Devitt, who'd supported me during my recovery, administered the oath of office and presented a copy of his "Ten Commandments for the New Judge" to me. The first commandment resonated the most: "be kind." These words would echo throughout my time on the bench. His commandment made me recall the burn unit. I'd been wholly reliant on the care team. Some of the staff were cold and impersonal, simply doing their jobs, while the kindness of others—the nursing assistant who brushed my hair, the young resident who stopped to visit with me, the nurse who encouraged me to run a marathon—left a lifelong impression on my heart and in my mind. Compassion became my guiding principle. Sooner than

I'd imagined, I'd have the opportunity to practice compassion in my own life. The adoption was coming through.

At long last, a month after my judgeship, Children's Home Society had a referral. The call came 15 months after we'd applied. Four-month-old Eun Joo Yoon would be arriving in just a few days. Minutes after receiving the call, the agency emailed her photo to us, and we immediately bonded with her. Reality set in—she was going to be our daughter, and we'd be her parents. "What shall we name her?" I asked Chuck. We decided on Sarah after my paternal grandmother. Then I hurried to call our family and friends to share the exciting news while Chuck cracked open a bottle of champagne.

Life can sometimes be complicated. A short while later, we received another call. Sarah's premature birth, coupled with the way her eyes appeared, hinted at a brain developmental anomaly. Sarah was in Korea, 6,207 miles away; how could we assess her condition? The hour moved at a snail's pace before we received a third call from our social worker. She told us a delegation of American military doctors, including a pediatrician, would be touring the Korean referral agency that day and had agreed to examine Sarah. Hope emerged, as did more questions. How competent were the military doctors? Should we trust them without seeing her ourselves? We took turns assuring each other, praying that if it was meant to be, we'd become her parents. A few panic-laden hours later, the agency called with a message from the doctors in Korea. Chuck and I squeezed each other's hands as we listened to their report. "Congratulate the new parents. She's the cutest, smartest little girl we've ever seen, and they're lucky to be her parents." I'd always prided myself on being stoic. I was reserved and undemonstrative, but becoming a mother moved me to tears. Our social worker assured us that the military medical team's credentials had been confirmed. Sarah was ours. With that, we knew we'd do everything to bring her home to us. Overwhelmed with joy and relief, Chuck and I awaited her arrival.

On November 11, 1982, a snowy Minnesota day, we drove to the airport to meet Sarah. Just four months old, she'd made the long flight to Seattle then to Minneapolis, escorted by representatives from the adoption agency. Over 40 of our family members and friends were waiting to see her at the airport, clutching balloons and bouquets of flowers. When the plane landed at a gate, the area bustled with activity. My focus remained fixed on the jetway, searching for that one special little face, as passengers began to disembark the plane. After what felt like hours, a woman approached me, cradling a little bundle wrapped in a yellow blanket. I couldn't believe the moment had arrived. I was going to be a mother.

Although I'd never been as excited for anything in my life as I was for the arrival of this baby, terror began to grip me. But when I slowly took Sarah into my arms, my fear about whether I was ready for motherhood dissipated. "Welcome home, Sarah," I whispered, taking hold of her olive-sized fist. The world around me faded, leaving just my baby daughter and me. Sarah was a living, breathing miracle. She looked up at me with her dark, curious eyes, so alert, aware of her surroundings, and seemingly unfazed by the crowd that had gathered to welcome her. I couldn't take my eyes off her tiny face. Once I took her in my arms, she seemed to belong there, and my heart was full with the feeling that we were meant to be together.

Amidst this overwhelming joy and celebration, there were the practicalities of life to consider. The day after Sarah's arrival, I was scheduled to go back to work. Sarah's arrival coincided with Veteran's Day, which had afforded me a holiday from work and the time to meet her flight. I'd only been serving as a judge for about a month, and taking parental leave was not feasible. Torn between my duties as a newly appointed judge and my responsibilities as a new parent, I didn't anticipate the internal struggle that ensued.

Before the plane crash, I was utterly dedicated to my work, often the last to leave the office, frequently devoting most of my weekends to working on cases. However, the accident had changed me, and so did becoming a mother. When Sarah joined our family, I wanted to be present for all aspects of her life—feeding her, playing with her, witnessing every stage of her development. At the same time, my desire to do meaningful work in the world was still strong. Like for many working mothers, my profound love for Sarah precipitated a delicate dance between my family obligations and the demands of my career.

A perfectionist in my professional life, I expected the same standards in my role as a mother. Perfectionism caught up with me at every turn, and the pressure I put on myself seemed to be sucking the joy out of me. Something had to give. These traits were a legacy from my mother so I sought her advice and wisdom. On a cold morning, I drove to her home and we sat together at Mom's breakfast nook with plates of scrambled eggs, toast, and orange juice before us. Sarah stirred, hiccupped gently, then fell back asleep in my arms. I broached my concerns. "How did you do it, Mom? You're as much of a perfectionist as I am. How did you manage when parenting Jim and me?" Hesitating while my mother poured another cup of coffee, I admitted, "I'm struggling and need your help."

Mom's eyes reflected a deep understanding borne of experience. She took my hand and said, "Perfectionism can be a double-edged sword, honey. While it can help you strive for excellence, it also comes with unrealistic expectations about parenting. You'll need to accept the imperfections."

I wiped away the tears rolling down my cheeks. "When I'm at the office, all I can think about is Sarah. And when I'm home, I feel guilty that I'm not working."

"Parenting, I think, is about guiding, supporting, and loving your children, not about being flawless. It's important not to push yourself so hard that you lose the ability to be present with Sarah. Because I love you, I want to tell you that you'll also need to make time for yourself as difficult as that will be for you."

Mom's words remained with me. Another shift in my perspective, I'd have to balance personal expectations with the realities of raising children. Juggling my career and parenthood, I realized I would have to consciously remind myself when I headed home that I'd need to leave the courtroom behind to be with my precious daughter. Releasing the grip of perfectionism proved challenging. Whenever I got caught up in self-criticism over the choices I was making, I tried to practice some self-compassion and asked myself "What's the most loving way I can treat myself right now?"

I knew it'd take time to accept that perfectionism in my parenting and in my profession was unrealistic. Slowly I tried to accept myself without judgment, and I learned the importance of asking for help and of delegating tasks, both at work and at home. I began to make time for activities that rejuvenated my mind and body, and I practiced mindfulness and journaled to help me process my emotions and gain clarity. Self-care became crucial to maintaining a balance in life. I didn't do that perfectly either, but the exercises helped me nurture a kinder, more forgiving relationship with myself in my attempt to manage the complexities of my dual responsibilities with greater ease.

Despite these efforts, a mere two weeks after experiencing the miracle of motherhood, we had another hurdle to overcome. I'd previously scheduled corrective surgery for my right hand during Thanksgiving break, not anticipating that Sarah would be arriving when she did. The surgery was essential to restore the functionality of my scarred hand. But now I am a new mother. How would I grapple with my own health issues? I yearned to be a pillar of strength for my baby, but I'd be temporarily incapacitated, unable to perform even the most basic tasks such as changing her diapers, dressing her, or preparing her bottles. I told myself that I'd still be able to cradle Sarah close to my heart, feel the warmth of her tiny body against mine, and feed her with my left hand. But once again, I'd be dependent upon family members' support, leaning on them for everything else. My reliance on them brought me back to those weeks after the crash when I needed their assistance for all the basic activities of daily living. I knew how blessed I was to have a husband and parents who would help with every diaper change, late-night feeding, and daily care that Sarah needed.

I returned to the occupational therapist for endless daily sessions. The exercises, stretches, and working with weights improved my strength and dexterity, and my hand slowly healed following my surgery. After a few weeks, my therapist asked, "Sheryl, you've come so far. Your hand is about 95 percent there. Isn't this good enough?"

"No," I retorted. "Regaining full use of my hand is imperative to me. I want 100 percent." Perhaps this was a bit abrupt and revealed my perfectionism, but I changed therapists to gain that extra five percent of hand function.

Describing my parents as "all in" on the grandparenting role would be a colossal understatement. The moment Dad saw her, she was his granddaughter in every sense of the word. Both Mom and Dad embraced Sarah's arrival with unparalleled enthusiasm, and they tried to spend every moment they could with her. They showered Sarah with love and attention transporting me back to my own childhood when my parents did the same for my brother and me. Mom, a highly educated individual with a keen intellect and an insatiable intellectual curiosity, had made the deliberate choice to stay at home. There was no question as to her commitment to our well-being, but I sensed she lived out her ambitions through my brother and me. She'd had high expectations of us. She encouraged us, perhaps even pushed us, toward achievements and paths she'd envisioned for herself. Later, I understood the weight of her unfulfilled dreams and wondered what she could have achieved had she continued her own career. With this in mind, I pledged to try to retain my identity, to pursue my dreams, and to be present for my children while still pursuing my professional goals.

My father's commitment to family also ran deep. His business was open 24 hours a day, seven days a week, and it wasn't uncommon for my father to work nights and weekends. However, he never missed a school or scouting event or sporting occasion in which we kids were involved. He unfailingly made it home every night because dinner with our family was nonnegotiable. Dad personified unwavering dedication to both family and to hard work, and these values were instilled in me.

When Sarah had been living with us just a month, we got an unexpected call. The other adoption agency to which we'd applied had a baby boy to place in our home. We knew we wanted Sarah to have a baby brother, but we were totally caught off guard and unprepared to parent two infants at the same time. After a candid conversation with the agency explaining our situation, the social worker agreed to put our application on hold for a two-year period—a much needed pause to get ready both mentally and emotionally to welcome another baby into our home. During that time, we fully embraced our time with Sarah—taking her on bicycle rides, introducing her to the joys of music, taking her to Bible and Sunday School, and starting to teach her how to swim. I'd often ask Sarah's caregiver to bring her to meet me at a playground near the courthouse during lunch hours so we could have a picnic and play together.

We still needed to take the steps to finalize her adoption and her legal status in this country. Although I felt Sarah was my daughter from the first moment I held her in my arms, these processes were necessary to ensure that she was legally recognized as a member of our family. Several weeks following placement, we finalized Sarah's adoption before my judicial colleague. After several months passed, Sarah had been living in the United States the requisite amount of time to become an American citizen. Judge Devitt, my mentor and friend who'd been so significant to my recovery, held a private session for us in his chambers, and we took the oath of citizenship on her behalf.

Chuck and I became a parenting team. He'd grown up around younger siblings preparing him to take on the role of a hands-on parent. We were both in the legal profession and supported each other in balancing our professional responsibilities with parenting. The demands of our respective careers though left little personal time. I functioned on less sleep than Chuck did, but he made the most of his time awake. As Sarah grew, the ticking clock constantly reminded us there never seemed to be enough hours in the day to do it all.

At bedtime when Sarah's gentle breathing indicated she was fast asleep, I'd delve into the work I'd brought home. Typically, my lights would go out after midnight and I'd wake up to the alarm at 5:30 the next morning. I never lost sight of my role as a parent, but physical exhaustion became my constant companion. Those years were a blur of courtroom battles and bedtime stories, of legal contests and school field trips, and they were years of learning to balance and prioritize many duties. The sacrifices and tireless efforts were worth it. I knew I was upholding the law and at the same time setting an example for Sarah.

Two years passed in the blink of an eye. My parents moved to the Twin Cities just after Sarah turned two and bought a large home near us where our family would spend quality time. When the agency called again, wanting to know if we were ready to welcome a baby boy into our family, we eagerly said, "Yes" without a moment's hesitation. We were excited that Sarah was going to become a big sister. Choosing his name was easy. There was a practice spanning several generations in my husband's family to name the firstborn son Charles Thomas. We continued this tradition. On February 25, 1985, Charlie came to live with us at the age of six weeks—two and a half months younger than Sarah was when she joined our family. When I held Charlie in my arms at the adoption agency, I noticed how incredibly tiny and fragile he seemed compared to Sarah when I first held her. He required a different kind of attention. We had to quickly learn the ropes of caring for such a young infant, our time filled with sleepless nights, endless diaper changes, and soothing lullabies, while we marveled at his every move and milestone.

Charlie was a bundle of energy. With that enthusiasm came a penchant for accidents. During those early years, it felt like we had a membership card with his name on it at the local emergency room. My blood ran cold when Charlie, at age two, picked up my hot curling iron. I'd turned away for just a second, and in that fleeting moment, he reached for it with innocent curiosity. The searing heat touched his delicate skin, and I watched in horror as it burned his tiny arm.

My mind raced to the worst-case scenarios. I called the only person I knew who could help me—Dr. Solem. When he answered the phone that Saturday afternoon, I could barely get the words out through my sobs to let him know why I was calling. He offered to meet us at the burn clinic so he could assess the injury. Charlie's pain was a language I understood all too well—one I wished he never had to speak. I felt gripped with an overwhelming sense of guilt. Each grimace, each small, muffled cry of discomfort he uttered caused me a deep sense of helplessness that I'd been unable to protect someone I loved from being burned. Fighting my own demons was one thing, but the simple fact that I could not take his place was brutal.

After examining Charlie's arm, Dr. Solem indicated that the burn wasn't severe, would not require skin grafting, and should heal naturally with time. Grateful that my son wouldn't need surgery like I did, it was devastating to think of the pain he was suffering. I applied an ointment Dr. Solem prescribed to aid the healing process and put a compression sleeve over the burned area to help prevent scarring. As I watched Charlie's little arm slowly heal, I counted my blessings that his injury hadn't been more severe. His arm completely healed within a month, leaving no lasting scars. But the memory of his pain and the shock in his eyes still fills me with a lingering regret and a profound sense of guilt.

Sheryl Ramstad

I chaired my brother Jim's campaigns for 30 years

My first Mother's Day as a new mom to my daughter Sarah

Sarah became an American citizen before Judge Devitt with our family in attendance

Sheryl Ramstad

Kristina's naturalization ceremony

Living Life Full Throttle

My entire family including my husband Lee Larson

CHAPTER 7
Committed To Healing

After the crash, I became singularly focused on healing, not just in terms of my physical recovery, but in every aspect of my life. I realized that true healing isn't just about fixing problems or mending what is broken. It has to encompass recovery, growth, and a path toward wholeness.

Consequently, for me it had an additional dimension to restore others. My commitment to this journey led me to engage with the Phoenix Society for Burn Survivors as a volunteer. Their *Survivors Offering Assistance in Recovery* or *SOAR* program would be a way for me to help others who, like me, had endured catastrophic burn injuries.

In 1984, at the World Burn Congress, I received specialized peer support training to prepare me.

This training enabled me to connect with burn survivors and with their loved ones, including those hospitalized in the same burn unit where I'd once been a patient. Going back there was emotional, and at the same time it felt as if I was coming full circle. Through *SOAR* interactions, I would offer not just practical advice but also encouragement to persevere through the recovery process. I wanted to return what I'd received during my own recovery—understanding, hope, and connection.

One patient stands out. I was asked to meet with a burn survivor who'd been injured in a gasoline explosion. An avid runner before the accident, she was extremely worried about whether she'd ever be able to run again. We talked through her fears and her desire to reclaim that part of her life. I shared my own experience with physical recovery, bringing photos from the marathons I'd run to reinforce for her the fact that healing is a journey often requiring patience and faith in the body's resilience.

Another patient I'd worked with, a young woman, had fallen into a campfire leaving her with significant burns. She confided in me that she was anxious about how the scars might affect her relationship with her boyfriend, who'd stayed by her bedside throughout her hospitalization. We spoke about the emotional and psychological challenges of adjusting to a new self-image, and I encouraged her to communicate openly with her partner. I told her that I understood how challenging that would be, that I didn't share my innermost concerns with Chuck and soon came to regret not being open with him. I reminded her that true love is not dependent on outward appearance but on the strength of connection and shared experience.

During these meetings, my message was always clear: survivors do not have to go through the physical, emotional, or social journey alone. I emphasized that a network of support is available from people like me who have survived similar traumatic injuries and walked the same difficult path to recovery.

Just as *SOAR* enabled me to focus on helping others heal, the judgeship profoundly transformed my career. In my previous role as a lawyer, I'd often been immersed in the adversarial tug-of-war that defines the legal system. However, stepping into the role of a judge shifted my perspective completely. My new role was no longer about winning or losing but about listening to people's concerns and administering justice with fairness and empathy. Every day, I was acutely aware of the real and lasting impact that my decisions could have on the lives of people who stood before me. Conflict is inevitable, but I learned that commitment to healing transcends psychological, physical, and spiritual causes of pain at all levels. What gratified me most wasn't the prestige or the authority that came with being a judge, but the opportunity to make a real difference in people's lives, to help restore them. Each person who appeared before me was dependent upon the decisions I made, just as I had been completely reliant upon the care of others as a burn patient.

I'll never forget an experience that happened close to Christmas. A defendant, charged with theft, stood before me in court accused of stealing some toys and food. "I'm guilty, your honor," he said in a shaky voice. "I had no money for food or Christmas gifts for my five children." His despair was immediately visible. I knew he was not a hardened criminal, but a desperate man driven to the edge by poverty. He'd committed petty theft to provide some Christmas joy for his family.

"Well, sir, I understand your intention was to provide for your family," I said. "There are community resources like food shelves and *Toys for Tots*, which would have been better alternatives. However, I'll give you a second chance. If you stay clear of the court system for six months, your charge will be dismissed." I motioned for his attorney to come forward. I quietly handed him some money for his client to buy a Christmas tree, gifts to put beneath it, and some food. It was a drop in the bucket. By showing concern and respect for his circumstances, I hoped it helped the healing process. Each year at Christmas, even decades later, I receive a holiday card from that attorney with the same message: "It's just not Christmas until I send my card to you. Your act of kindness lasts a lifetime."

Another case I had as a judge has stayed with me, too. One afternoon, my law clerk informed me that a young couple called to ask what I would charge to officiate at their wedding. They'd approached another judge who said he'd perform the wedding for $500, but that was beyond their means. I told my clerk to let them know that $50 would be enough for my services. On the day of their wedding, I asked the groom to place a ring on his bride's finger. Looking down at the floor, he said sadly and with embarrassment, "Your honor, I have no ring because I couldn't afford one."

Reacting quickly, I congratulated them both and said, "Sir, please take the money you intended to pay me and buy a ring in honor of the vows you just made." Seeing their joyful faces remains a cherished memory and reinforced that a small gesture of kindness can have a lasting impact on the lives of others. Quite simple, yet so meaningful for the recipients.

I longed to do more. I'll never forget how important the compassion of strangers was to me when I needed it most—the commercial pilot who witnessed my crash and not only walked me away from the burning cockpit but remained with me until the paramedics arrived. The former Republic Airlines pilot who visited me in the burn unit, sharing his own experience having been badly burned in a plane crash. To help restore others by paying these kindnesses forward became a goal of mine. When I could connect with people who appeared before me on a human level, it brought home to me the impact the legal system can have on the lives of others. I was drawn toward finding work that would correspond with my personal ethos—helping people put their lives back together despite their involvement in contentious conflicts. This led me to an unusual and consequential decision: to request a transfer to Family Court.

"Are you sure you're willing to step into a world where heartache is as prevalent as the paperwork?" the Chief Judge asked. "You know that Family Court isn't a popular assignment among judges because it can be messy. The disputes dredge up despair, anger, and rarely, joy. And the child custody disputes can be heart-wrenching. Why do you want to be transferred there?"

"Truthfully, Chief, I am drawn to these very challenges. Something within me shifted following my accident, so I now want to alleviate the inherent adversarial nature of legal proceedings. A restorative, more conciliatory approach could transform the way parties handle their sensitive disputes. It is not despite, but because of, these challenges that I am drawn to the Family Court—to foster a courtroom that embraces reconciliation over recrimination."

"Well, Sheryl, don't say I didn't tell you so. But if you desire to inject a dose of humanity into the proceedings, I'm not going to stop you."

Many viewed Family Court as a maelstrom of drama. Surely a different courtroom environment was possible—one that replaced blame with one focused on healing. Though rare in the legal world, I believed this attitude could be transformative. Why couldn't Family Court become a more solution-focused arena, one that prioritized resolving disputes constructively over battling for revenge?

For me, a case that exemplified this shift involved a well-known and highly respected businessman. His adult daughter claimed that he had fondled her during her childhood, and years later, she sought to restrict his rights to see his grandchildren. She threatened to report the decades old incidents to the police. This revelation could shatter his reputation as a successful entrepreneur, community leader, and loving family man. It had become a family crisis. The siblings were torn apart, some sided with her while others staunchly defended their father. The family was in turmoil, on the brink of irreparable damage, and a court ruling would not mend the rifts that had formed.

Recognizing the potential long-term implications of a public hearing, I steered them away from going to trial. Instead, I proposed mediation, offering to facilitate the discussions myself. After days of challenging negotiations, we reached a settlement. It was comprehensive, confidential, and considerate of all parties involved including, most importantly, the children. Providing supervised visitations for the grandfather would ensure the well-being and safety of his grandchildren while maintaining a significant connection with them. This resolution focused on the long-term reconciliation within the family, not only the immediate crisis, and the outcome reinforced my belief in the importance of addressing such disputes with empathy, understanding, and a focus on reuniting families.

In my new role, I found myself not just administering justice, but also guiding parties toward constructive resolutions. I encouraged estranged spouses and feuding parents to step back from their contentiousness and consider the greater good of their family, especially when children were caught in the emotional crossfire. As a new mother, I knew only too well the impact on them. Some individuals clung fiercely to their grievances, their hurt turning to bitterness. They insisted on a take-no-prisoners approach to litigation. But to my relief and satisfaction, many were receptive to a more amicable process and were willing to engage in civilized discourse.

Each individual who appeared before me carried their own unique story, their own burdens and fears. Whether it was a family seeking resolution, an individual looking for justice, or a community facing the aftermath of a crime, I realized that their futures rested on the decisions I made. In many ways, it mirrored my own journey—just as I had relied on others to help me rebuild my life, they were looking to me to help them navigate the complexities of the legal system, and, in some cases, begin their own journey of healing. This responsibility weighed heavily on me as I strove to bring the same empathy and thoughtfulness to my role as a judge that I'd once needed from those around me during my recovery. I knew firsthand how critical it was to feel heard, understood, and supported, and I carried that awareness with me in every case I presided over.

In 1985, after nearly four years on the bench, and now newly parenting my second infant Charlie, I found myself increasingly drained by the adversarial climate in court. Strife and rancor still pervaded and seemed to me to be unnecessary and destructive. It became clear that allowing parties to actively participate in resolving their conflicts outside of the courtroom had profound value. I began to champion mediation, recognizing that it empowered parties to forge their own agreements with the precision and care of skilled artisans, as opposed to the blunt force wielded by judicial decrees.

An offer to fulfill this dream came in 1986. I was approached by Rider Bennett, a renowned Twin Cities law firm known for its legal acumen and for its culture of civility, community involvement, and client-centeredness. My decision to join the firm marked a pivotal shift in my career, steering me toward a more conciliatory legal practice that I long aspired to. There, I was able to work as a mediator, handling myriad disputes—everything from intellectual property issues and commercial conflicts to personal injury cases, estate matters, and healthcare disagreements. The work proved to be incredibly fulfilling.

An especially acrimonious estate case involved a father who left an extensive amount of valuable land to his children when he died. Distrust among siblings was profound because of underlying family dynamics involving alcoholism, sexual abuse, and physical and mental illness. Shortly before the mediation, I received a call from the attorneys who represented the siblings, asking, "Does your office have a metal detector to scan everyone before entering the mediation room? We wanted to alert you that the family dynamics could erupt into violence during the mediation." Their troubled past and longstanding breakdown in communication had evidently been suppressed until the father's passing. Now a storm of contentiousness had been unleashed. Each sibling vied for a piece of the estate as if it were compensation for the affection they missed from their father, which they felt had always eluded them. To me, their inheritance fight seemed less about material assets than a contest for acknowledgement of the deprivation they experienced while their father was alive.

The mediation was scheduled to last several days. Initially it looked like the dispute would be bitter and irreparable. To my surprise, a huge shift occurred by the end of the first day. The siblings, once hostile, left the proceedings arm in arm. I heard one sibling say as he left my office, "I'm so sorry we didn't get together before this so we could have avoided many years of anguish." Through mediation, what began as a battle for their father's legacy evolved into a conciliatory journey. This alternative to litigation allowed the parties to mend their fractured relationships, healing the familial bonds that had been severed by years of hurt and disagreement. In my practice, I witnessed how mediation can resolve disputes effectively, offering remedies that rarely take place in confrontational legal settings.

The misunderstandings I encountered in my work seeped into our personal life. I was disturbed by the biases of others, and we grappled with the often insensitive comments made. When we met people who saw fair-skinned and blue-eyed Charlie next to his Korean-born sister, some would refer to him as "our own" child. The assumption was clear—Charlie shared the blond hair and blue-eyed Scandinavian features of my husband and me, suggesting to them that he hadn't been adopted, whereas Sarah obviously was. I certainly let them know that both Charlie and Sarah were "my own" children in every sense of the word from the first moment I held them in my arms. I wondered why people insinuated that adoption is a second-rate form of parenting. This notion is deeply flawed. Adoption is intentional parenting, and we chose it consciously and wholeheartedly rather than by default. It was the right path for our family given our circumstances, and my love for our children is unconditional. Life without them is unimaginable, and I wanted to shield them from unkind perceptions and remarks of others. Reasoned intervention would be my course of action at home and at work.

At a time when litigation was the norm, I embarked on a mission to introduce mediation as a viable and effective alternative. I thought my role as an educator would be key. While I was working at the firm, I was hired by William

Mitchell School of Law to teach mediation part time to law students. Challenging their conventional adversarial mindsets, I encouraged them to consider mediation as a harmonious and collaborative approach to dispute resolution. Through my lectures, I hoped to inspire a new generation of legal professionals who'd embrace mediation.

My efforts extended beyond the classroom. I opted to teach continuing education seminars to reach seasoned lawyers and to tout the advantages of mediation. During these sessions, I illustrated how mediation could provide disputants the opportunity to heal and to foster more satisfying long-term outcomes than traditional litigation. I also spread the word about mediation's positive impact through articles I wrote for legal publications. Soon, mediation gained traction within the legal profession and among the public. Retired judges began offering their services as mediators for hire.

Mediation transitioned from a fringe concept to a mainstream practice, and it was a significant milestone for me, too. I felt good about being part of this transformative journey. I would compare it to my own journey from crash victim to survivor, courtroom combatant to a conciliatory healer, and of course evolving in a parallel way, mediation became a reality.

When Sarah turned four in 1986, she began expressing her strong desire for a sister. She'd become aware of the racial differences between herself and her younger brother. "When Charlie gets older, he'll look like you, but I'll look different." It hurt me to hear her express what I'd heard from insensitive strangers. Charlie's blond hair and blue eyes somehow impacted her sense of belonging to and identifying with our family. Around that time, a little boy in Sarah's preschool class called her "China Face." Sarah tearfully told us that she didn't want to go to school anymore. Trying to rectify the situation, I purchased a book for the class and one for the little boy's family that emphasized the beauty of differences and diversity. With the passage of time and a lot of reinforcement both at home and from her teacher, Sarah began to adjust and to feel more comfortable in her own skin.

Sarah's plea for a sister struck a deeply personal chord within me. I was very close to my older brother; however, I'd always wanted a sister. Now that I was a parent myself, I had the opportunity to fulfill that dream for Sarah. She was four and Charlie two. My husband and I thought we were ready to welcome another child into our family. The adoption paperwork was easier this time because we were familiar with the process. Moreover, I'd been serving as pro bono legal counsel for the adoption agency, so I knew the staff who would help with our placement.

We were keenly aware that adoptions from South Korea were becoming increasingly more difficult. As the 1988 Seoul Summer Olympics approached, international adoption of South Korean children became the focus of global attention and a propaganda tool for North Korea. They accused South Korea of selling its children to foreigners because they couldn't provide for them. As a result, South Korea threatened to end international adoptions and to keep adoptions domestic.

The uncertainty surrounding our application to adopt an infant daughter from Korea left us in a constant state of anxiety. Although the agency believed that adopting a sister for Sarah might still be possible, they warned us about the uncertain political situation. The wait could be much longer than we'd experienced with Sarah's referral. We agreed to move forward, clinging to the hope that by the time Sarah entered kindergarten, she'd have a baby sister.

Waiting for the adoption agency's referral call was like watching a single drop of water drip slowly down a windowpane. Finally, after months of uncertainty, the call came. A New Year's baby! Kim Hwa Rhee, born on January 1, 1988, would be joining our family. Her photo showed an alert, darling little girl with shocks of black hair. On May 6, 1988, our new daughter, Kristina, entered our lives. When Sarah, filled with pride and love, asked us to bring Kristina to "sharing time" at school to introduce her new baby sister to her kindergarten class, my heart melted.

Kristina's arrival was like none other. At the time, adoptive parents were allowed to travel to Korea to escort their babies back to Minnesota. Of course, I wanted to go, but the thought of leaving Sarah and Charlie and my commitments made it impossible for me to do so. I was extremely busy with my responsibilities at work and teaching, which I couldn't abandon when the phone call would come letting us know we could pick up our daughter. My mother, trained as a medical social worker, understood the adoption process well. I asked my parents if they'd like to go to Korea to bring Kristina home. They agreed, excited to be able to be the first to have a glimpse of their newest grandchild and to share the flight from Seoul to Minneapolis with her. A few weeks later, they departed for Korea. The timing couldn't have been more perfect. Kristina was scheduled to arrive on Uncle Jim's birthday.

My older brother and only sibling, Jim, and I were four years apart. I looked up to him, and he, in turn, was very protective of me. It seemed normal that I would chair his campaigns for the Minnesota State Senate and the United States Congress over the years. Our connection deepened even further when Chuck and I started our family. Jim's chosen path in politics meant he was unmarried and had no children of his own. He doted on Sarah and Charlie with as much love as was humanly possible. When we welcomed Kristina into our family on Jim's 42nd birthday, he couldn't contain his excitement. He was the first to arrive at the airport and eagerly awaited her flight's arrival.

By the time the flight finally touched down, Mom and Dad were exhausted. Their journey from Korea entailed two grueling flights, totaling over 20 hours, during which they hadn't slept a wink. When Mom disembarked, Uncle Jim presented her with a dozen long-stemmed red roses, and Charlie and Sarah eagerly stood by with a teddy bear to give to their baby sister. Mom lovingly placed Kristina in my arms. I noticed she had small pieces of paper safety-pinned all over her—on her diaper, her sleeper, and her blanket. On them in my mother's careful handwriting I found Kristina's name. "We wanted to make sure that nobody on the plane switched babies on us, so I pinned her name on her clothes, and we stayed awake all night watching her sleep."

As a bachelor, I recall Jim never took care of infants, but he was looking over my shoulder the entire time I held Kristina. He coached me every step of the way. "Sheryl, hold her head; put your hand behind her neck. Be careful or you'll drop her. I think she might be hungry; where's her bottle?" Once an older brother, always an older brother. Teaching me the ropes of parenthood, he'd somehow transformed into an instant baby expert. When he held Kristina in his arms, his eyes expressed the deep love he had for her, just as he had for Sarah and Charlie.

My husband Chuck waited patiently for his turn to hold Kristina. He was just as excited as the rest of us when Kristina arrived, and his years of experience as an older brother to five siblings, combined with his years of parenting Sarah and Charlie, had more than prepared him to be an active and engaged presence in Kristina's life. He readily took on many of the daily responsibilities of driving to day care, going to doctors' appointments, and ensuring that birthdays were special occasions. Chuck's approach to fatherhood was one of consistent love and care. When it came to our children, he was always there for them, no matter what the situation, and he offered unwavering support and guidance at every step.

After all the excitement of Kristina's arrival died down a bit, Dad told us about an unexpected scene at the Seattle airport. When their flight from Seoul landed and passengers were required to go through U.S. Customs, my parents were directed to a line for U.S. citizens, while Kristina was supposed to go through a different line designated for foreigners. Airport personnel offered to hold her to allow my parents to go through their line, but my mother was adamant. "I'm not letting go of her. You can arrest me if you want, but I'm going to keep her with me until we deliver her to my daughter's family in Minneapolis." Somehow Kristina was allowed to remain in their arms as they proceeded through the customs line.

Mom and Dad participated in all aspects of our children's lives—school events, doctors' appointments, birthday celebrations, and ball games, they were always there. Whenever Chuck and I had conflicts, they would welcome the children into their home, feeding them homemade macaroni and cheese and making them feel right at home. But when Kristina turned five, things began to change.

In 1993, I was the parent of three young children trying to maintain an active career. Then an unexpected family situation caught me totally by surprise. At 8 a.m. on Easter Sunday morning, my mother called me, frantically saying, "I woke up restless last night and picked up the picture I have on my dresser. I looked on the back, and I saw 'I love you' and that it was signed 'Sheryl'. I couldn't remember who was in the picture." Mom told me she'd called her cousin in Kansas City in the middle of the night to find out who 'Sheryl' was.

I never expected our lives to change so drastically in a manner of moments. Although her memory had been deteriorating for some time, nothing had prepared me for this. The woman who'd brought me into this world, who'd always been at my side, didn't know who I was. A proud and fiercely independent woman, my mother had been covering up her memory issues, blaming them on the fact that she was hard of hearing. Her condition could no longer be ignored. I wished I could have reached out through the phone to hug her.

We took Mom to Rochester, Minnesota, to see a Mayo Clinic neurologist. He conducted several tests and discussed the results with us. "The tests strongly suggest that Mrs. Ramstad has Alzheimer's disease." Dr. Petersen told us it's a progressive disorder that cannot be healed in the traditional sense. A multifaceted approach to manage her symptoms and improve her quality of life would help, but wouldn't cure her. I listened carefully to each word he was saying, hoping my intense focus on the doctor would keep the scream from building in my throat and escaping. My mother, once a pillar of strength and self-sufficiency, had always been the embodiment of resilience—smart, hard-working, and fiercely independent. Now, she was facing a precipitous journey into her own vulnerability and dependence.

I sought out every resource I could find to learn about Alzheimer's disease. Despite my numerous questions, the answers were few and far between. I wanted badly to find something or somebody to heal her. I also was determined to give her the same level of care she had provided me when I was burned and to proffer the love she showed our family. Yet I could only watch as Alzheimer's took hold, stripping her of her abilities, one by one, erasing her personality. Dad insisted on caring for her at home, and suffered two heart attacks while doing so. The long work hours, along with raising three children and caring for my parents, stretched me thin. Faced with the deterioration of the health of both my parents, I realized that while I couldn't cure them, I had to find a way to accept what was happening.

We implemented several lifestyle adjustments to ensure Mom's safety and comfort. We installed dead-bold locks on all the doors to prevent her from wandering off, used diapers at night to manage her incontinence, and organized home healthcare assistance. The assistance addressed Mom's physical needs and, thank goodness, provided emotional support for our family. I tried to help with activities of daily living which included things like bathing, toileting, and eating to lighten my father's load and to be there for Mom. Meanwhile,

Chuck and I grappled with managing our children's busy schedules, keeping track of their doctors' and dental appointments, getting them to practices, and making sure schoolwork was completed. I hadn't realized how much I'd depended on Mom's help.

Typically, I was the one who got my children to where they needed to be whether it was to school, to extracurricular activities, to playdates, or to school field trips with their classes, and I planned their birthday celebrations and the anniversaries of their arrival in this country. On Sarah and Kristina's *Arrival Days*, I went to their classrooms equipped with props such as Korean maps, fairy tales, photographs, and pear apples so their classmates would gain a better understanding of our daughters' Korean background. Since Charlie was born in the U.S., we chose themes such as baseball for his celebrations. One year on his *Arrival Day*, when he came home from school, he told me that some of his classmates said they wished they'd been adopted so they could have "two birthdays." We always told our children how fortunate we were to be their parents and stressed that their birth givers, unable to care for them, had demonstrated true love by ensuring that they would be raised in a family like ours. We hoped we'd given them a sense of security, knowing they were unconditionally loved.

My children were fascinated that my hands were different from theirs. On several occasions, as I reached for their small hands to guide them safely across the street, one of them would ask, "Why is your hand so wrinkled? Does it hurt? Tell me what happened." I turned their questions into teachable moments, explaining to them in an age-appropriate way how I got burned.

I tried to encourage my children to embrace adventure and to see how my own escapades had led me to incredible experiences, personal growth, and some formidable circumstances. "Do nothing in moderation," my motto, had thrust me into some extreme situations. To integrate my desire for my children to go into the world with lessons learned from my own past, I tried to make the point that when they'd attempt new activities, they should act responsibly and exercise great caution. None of my children developed a fear of flying, even after hearing the details of my plane crash and seeing the aftermath on my body. Instead, they seemed remarkably fearless, and they tackled new challenges with enthusiasm, believing that they could overcome any obstacle.

In 1998, when Sarah was 16, Charlie was 13, and Kristina turned 10, a group of politically active individuals approached me with an offer, "Sheryl, we want you to run for Hennepin County Attorney. You have experience as a prosecutor, a public defender, and as a judge and clearly are competent in the courtroom. We need you to bring your conciliatory approach to the County Attorney's Office." This was unexpected. While in private practice, it became evident to me that prosecutors often prioritized securing convictions over seeking true justice. It made me unhappy and dissatisfied, so I thought it was time for a change.

Initially, the thought of stepping into the role of a political candidate didn't appeal to me. My children were still in junior and senior high school, and it was challenging to keep up with their activities—baseball, softball, soccer, Girl Scouts, homework. I was torn. Could I be a good daughter and parent, while still contributing to the community in such a demanding position? The party activists urged me to consider the race, with assurances that they'd assist in the campaign. The more I thought about it, I began to see the chief prosecutor position as a potential means to mend fractures in the community and it could be an avenue to solve these dilemmas. My family and my law firm expressed support. "Mom, we'll help you," Sarah said. "We can get our friends to march in parades, hand out flyers, and tell their parents to vote for you." When Charlie and Kristina agreed, Chuck urged me to run, saying he'd be on board.

Being an active participant in the democratic process and an engaged citizen had been our family credo that was instilled in Jim and me by our parents and grandparents. They devoted time and resources to their community and supported political candidates, and they were involved in organizations like the American Legion Auxiliary. The fact that I grew up in a family in which public service was revered motivated me. With these considerations in mind, I decided to become a candidate.

For nearly 30 years, I had the privilege of chairing my brother Jim's political campaigns so I was no stranger to the political process. But it's one thing to oversee another person's campaign, and another to be the face of it. One step removed from the direct pressures encountered by the candidate, I didn't understand the stress, scrutiny, and personal toll on a candidate until I ran for office myself.

Running for Hennepin County Attorney turned out to be an incredibly tough and competitive battle. My opponent, Amy Klobuchar, began her campaign two years ahead of mine. This gave her a significant edge in terms of visibility and familiarity with voters. For several decades, Jim Klobuchar, Amy's father, had written a regular newspaper column in the *Minneapolis Star Tribune*, which gave her widespread name recognition. Although I'd been endorsed by both the Republican and the Reform parties, I hadn't grasped the enormity of the challenge in running against the dominant party in the county. This wasn't just a race against an individual opponent; it was a contest against the Democratic party's established political machinery, which gave my opponent vast resources and support.

I threw myself into the campaign despite the obstacles, but my commitment took an immense toll on my family and me. We worked around the clock. Chuck was my biggest supporter from the very beginning, encouraging me to pursue this difficult path. However, as it turned out, the same level of enthusiasm wasn't mirrored within the rest of our family.

Prior to the election, the weeks were filled with round-the-clock activities. The parades, leafletting, phone banks, and events in constant motion left our two younger children—Kristina, who was just 10 years old, and Charlie, who was 13—to fend for themselves much of the time. I remember Kristina asking me one evening as I was heading out to a political debate, "Mom, do you have to go out again? Can you please stay home with us tonight?" It tore at my heartstrings to tell her that I'd committed to the debate so I couldn't stay home with them. Sarah, our eldest at age sixteen, fared better. Her own interests and social life made it easier for her to navigate the campaign chaos and find her own space amidst it.

I saw my campaign as more than a political endeavor. The County Attorney position was an opportunity to take healing to a broader stage. I'd always advocated for policies and practices that aimed to prevent crime, to rehabilitate offenders, and to provide support for victims. I wanted to address the root causes of the issues and to promote a more compassionate and equitable society. In speeches, interactions with voters, and policies I proposed, I pledged to address issues of justice, fairness, and safety. It was my calling. This sense of duty soon became all-consuming, blinding me to the personal toll the months-long campaign was taking on my family. It left little room for the quality time that my children needed and deserved. The extended hours, constant travel, and relentless exhaustion wore me down. Distracted and preoccupied, I struggled to strike a balance between the demands of the campaign and my responsibilities as a daughter and a parent. Sometimes during lunch hours, I'd drive fifty miles to take food to my parents. Once I rushed from a fundraiser to a school Halloween party, changing in a gas station restroom out of my suit into a Care Bear costume.

The pursuit of responsible leadership was certainly important, but it should never have come at the expense of my children and our family. Even now, it presses hard on my heart knowing that there were moments when I should have been more present for my family, more attuned to the emotions and concerns of my children. This lesson would in the future influence my perspective on the choices I made in life.

The morning of Election Day arrived dreary and wet. A persistent drizzle turned the city into a sea of glistening pavement. I slogged through downtown and the suburbs, visiting polling places and shaking the cold, clammy hands of early voters whose faces were chilled by the wind. When I stopped by our phone banks, the scent of hot coffee and the occasional crinkle of snack wrappers filled the room while callers sat in rows, headsets on, tirelessly encouraging people to get out and vote. Outside, supporters braved the rain, holding campaign signs high on overhead walkways and bridges while shouting, "Vote today!" The sight of their drenched but determined faces bolstered my spirits.

After the polls closed, supporters gathered at the hotel ballroom where the room reverberated with a blend of hopeful murmurs and the clinking of glasses. Chuck, the kids, and I retreated to a private hotel room, where I paced incessantly, eyes glued to the television. The vote count updates sent spasms through me, the numbers crawling slowly across the bottom of the screen. For several hours, the race inched forward, the gap between my opponent and me never more than a few hundred votes. Commentators declared other races, their confident tones contrasting sharply with the repeated refrain that my race was too close to call.

Midnight approached, and I returned to the ballroom to let our weary and worn supporters know that the vote count would extend to the next day. They trickled out of the ballroom, their once hopeful cheers replaced by subdued goodbyes.

The oppressive silence and the weight of uncertainty pressed down on my family and me while we waited in our hotel room. We tried to sleep. I tossed and turned, my mind filled with thoughts of the race. When I did marathons, I could muster the energy to push myself further. But for this race, I felt impotent. It was now out of my hands. The minutes dragged on and amplified the heavy stillness of the night. How long before we'd know the results? The question, unanswered and unsettling, preoccupied me all night.

A knot of anxiety twisted in my stomach when I woke up in the morning, my eyes gritty from lack of sleep. I reached for my phone, but the screen showed no updates. The race still hung in the balance. It felt like I was waking up from a bad dream only to realize it wasn't over yet. My campaign manager called and suggested we take the team to lunch at a local sports bar. The idea of food seemed alien in my current state, but I agreed, hoping it might provide a distraction.

We went to a cozy, wood-paneled place where the comforting aroma of fried food and the murmur of lunchtime chatter greeted us. I felt a dozen pairs of eyes on me as I searched for a table on the far side of the room where a group of my dedicated campaign staff had gathered. They waved me over, their smiles strained, their faces reflecting exhaustion. Out of the corner of my eye, I saw Jesse Ventura approaching. I felt a pang of envy for the former professional wrestler who'd already crossed the finish line, his victory secured, while I was still stuck in limbo. Putting his hand on my shoulder, Minnesota's newly elected governor said, "Hey, Sheryl, we shocked the world, didn't we? How's your race going?"

"We sure did, Governor. Congratulations on your victory. My race is still too close to call so we're waiting for the final word."

"Well, let me tell you this: no matter what happens, there's a place for you in my administration. You've got way too much talent to waste. The people need you, and you belong in public service. It's in your DNA. So don't lose hope. Maybe the voters got it right; if not, your loss is my gain!"

"Thanks, Governor. I appreciate that. We'll be in touch."

Later that day the votes were finally tallied. I lost by half a percentage point, just short of victory. The suspense and the hope had lingered until the very end, and it made my eventual loss even more upsetting. Jesse Ventura's earlier comments rang in my ears. Even though I lost faith in myself, he believed in me. Somehow I would need to find the capacity to once again believe in myself.

Looking back, I can see that running for office, the ensuing campaign, and the defeat were integral to my healing. After my crash, I'd thrown myself into marathon training, career advancement, the courtroom, and building my family. During the campaign, I was completely absorbed in the pursuit of public service. This endeavor became so much more than winning an election as I'd doggedly pursued my commitment to bring healing into the community. Unfortunately, it came at a cost.

Amidst the chaos of my own life, the challenges of my recovery, the pressures of work, the never-ending household chores, and the countless duties of family, it would have been easy to feel we'd all missed out. In hindsight, when my children grew older, we had a chance to discuss how the campaign had impacted their lives. Sarah, Charlie, and Kristina had gained a greater understanding of the political process and the realities of running for office. At the same time, this exposure made them realize that none of them wanted to be involved in politics or to hold any public office ever. To this day, they have actively avoided anything related to politics, even innocuous events such as a parade.

Despite the difficulties they faced when I was a candidate, my children came to understand why I ran. They acknowledged they were proud of me. The campaign was a learning experience for all of us. The strong bond I share with each of my children speaks volumes of the foundation built on love, trust, and understanding we established during their formative years. And my accident, though a significant detour, led me to my greatest blessing—the adoption of three precious children whom I dearly love.

After the election and regardless of the outcome, little did we know that we were in store for other things, challenges we did not anticipate after the defeat.

Living Life Full Throttle

My brother, Jim, and I marched in parades together during the County Attorney campaign.

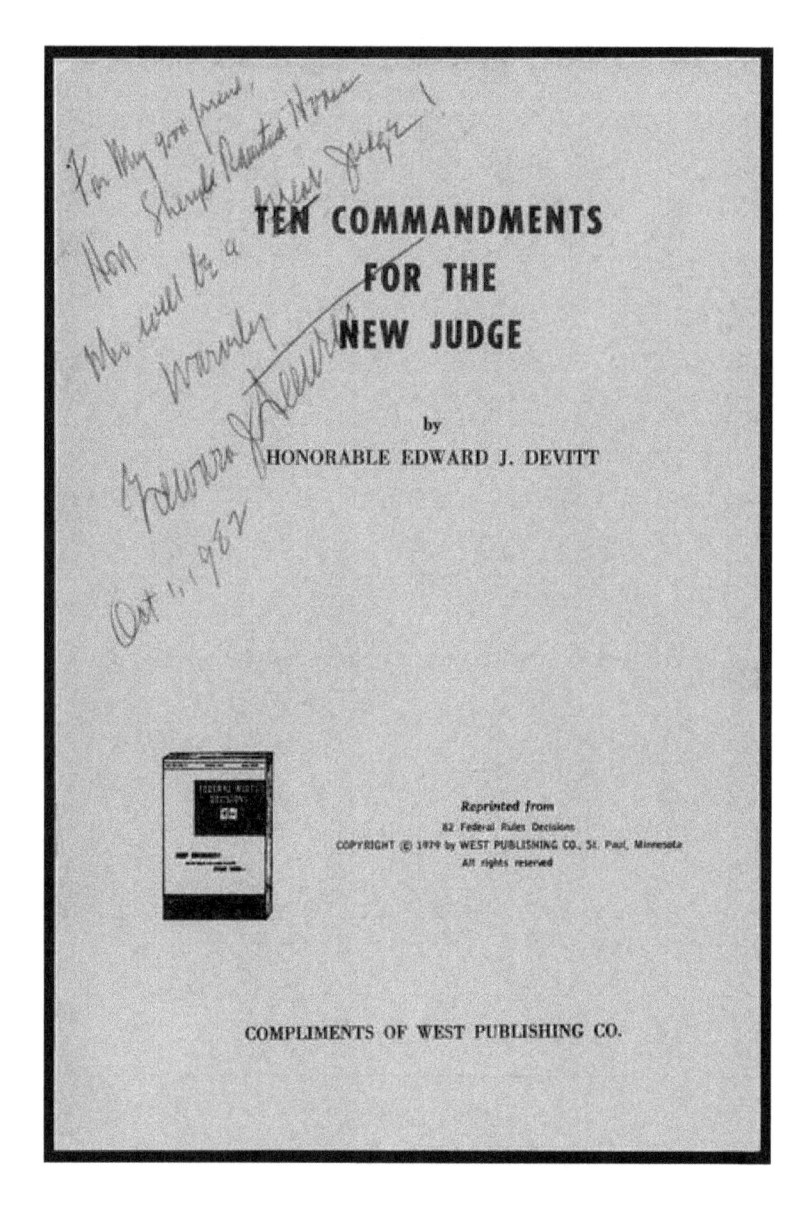

TEN COMMANDMENTS FOR THE NEW JUDGE

by

HONORABLE EDWARD J. DEVITT

Reprinted from
82 Federal Rules Decisions
COPYRIGHT © 1979 by WEST PUBLISHING CO., St. Paul, Minnesota
All rights reserved

COMPLIMENTS OF WEST PUBLISHING CO.

Judge Devitt's gift to me when he swore me in as a judge.

CHAPTER 8

When Losing Is Winning

The political atmosphere was highly charged in Minnesota when I ran for office in 1998. The candidacy of Jesse Ventura for Governor was seen as a curiosity and not a serious challenge. Coming from a significantly different background than the traditional political paths of his opponents, and as a candidate from the Reform Party, which had never had a major political victory in the state, his bid for governor looked like a long shot.

Ventura, born in 1951, an actor and television personality, was a member of the U.S. Navy Demolition Team during the Viet Nam War. He later became a professional wrestler and a bodyguard. Self-proclaimed Jesse.

"The Body", at six feet four and over 275 pounds, baldheaded, and with a deeply dimpled chin, Ventura was a formidable and controversial figure, who often lobbed outrageous statements such as "If you always tell the truth, you don't need a long memory" and "It's the people's money, stupid."

As the campaign unfolded, Ventura's straightforward though unorthodox style began to resonate with a segment of voters who were tired of traditional politics. Much to the surprise of political pundits and the public alike, his message and approach gained momentum. The turning point occurred at the State Fair that year, just a few months before the election. Several political candidates had set up booths at Minnesota's largest and most popular public gathering, but one booth stood out from the rest—Jesse Ventura's. When I walked past it, I could see his campaign merchandise—T-shirts, buttons, yard signs, bumper stickers, and other paraphernalia—flying off the shelves at an astonishing rate. Crowds hoped to gain a glimpse of the popular politician. Ventura's campaign caught fire with common citizens who appeared ready for change. His unique approach and appeal as an outsider offered them something different. By election day, the energy and excitement evident at the State Fair had spread across the state. Those who'd never voted before, who felt disillusioned with politics, were turning out to cast their ballots, many of them for the first time. The exit polls showed they'd cast their ballots for Ventura.

On election night, Ventura won, defying predictions and surprising the political establishment. At his victory party, wearing a pink feather boa, he exclaimed, "We shocked the world!" and it was true. Ventura's surge in popularity and his appeal to those outside the traditional voter base had changed the game entirely.

A few days before the election, the polls had indicated I was leading my opponent by five points among likely voters but the unlikely ones showed up to vote. I'd given my campaign everything I had: my heart, my soul, my time, my energy, and my effort. But in the end I'd lost. The weight was suffocating. I had no idea what to do next. When the crash occurred, I grappled with my shattered emotions and myriad questions. Now I was once again asking myself similar questions. "What happened?" "How can I put the pieces of my life back together again?"

Like then, I had no clear vision of a path forward, with the label LOSER across my forehead. Although there were no visible bandages or wounds this time, I was lost in a sea of "what ifs" and "if only." Trapped in a fog of regret and uncertainty, I was unable to break free from its grasp. One of the most painful things was that I'd let precious moments with my family slip away. Because of my preoccupation with the campaign, I'd missed simple joys such as watching my kids play ball, spending lazy days by the lake, and being present with them. Hijacked by the relentless demands of the campaign, my attention diverted, I'd been emotionally distant and unavailable to those who mattered most. And my professional life had hit a roadblock. I'd taken a hiatus from my law practice, which seemed like a necessary step at the time, but it left me in limbo with no clients or cases to return to. This uncertainty of my career amplified the sense of aimlessness and worry that pervaded my days.

After my accident I'd rebuilt my life, but would I have the energy to do it again? Would I have the resilience to embark on another journey of healing? Putting the pieces of my career back together would take strength I wasn't sure I had. I went through a period of soul-searching and introspection that involved peeling back layers of self-doubt and redefining my definition of success, no longer tied to winning cases or elections. I wondered whether returning to my law practice was the right direction to go, since my mission to help others heal had languished there. My family and friends reached out with kind words and emotional support, like Judge Devitt and others had done while I was hospitalized. Their efforts were a balm to my troubled soul, but the path forward remained uncertain. Struggling to find my way forward, I took long walks, hoping that nature would heal me. I went to church seeking serenity and perspective and sent up "arrow prayers," asking for God's grace and guidance.

After giving myself a six-week window to find my way, I realized that action was imperative. I decided to reach out to people, to engage in conversations about my future, and to seek their input on potential opportunities. To gain insight into my strengths and weaknesses, I underwent psychological testing, hoping it would illuminate the right path for me. Days turned into nights as I carefully combed through help wanted ads investigating employment prospects. With each passing day, I began to accept that true success meant to rise from defeat, to rebound from adversity, and to find new ways to fulfill the healing mission I felt compelled to do. I couldn't let the election results define me any more than the crash had. Moving through the despair took several weeks, but ultimately this perceived failure morphed into a significant personal victory. Life seemed to prove again—just like it did after the crash—that the greatest growth often comes from our hardest falls.

When Jesse Ventura, the new governor, announced that he was beginning to organize his administration, I submitted my application. I was eager to be part of a reform-minded team that focused on policy rather than politics. I hoped it'd be an answer to what I'd been searching for and would align with my vision of helping others. When the transition team informed me that I was under consideration for a position in Governor Ventura's Cabinet, a ray of light emerged. They asked which position interested me. I told them I thought my background in criminal law, coupled with the prison work I'd done early in my career, made me well suited for Commissioner of Corrections. Cabinet positions were highly sought after. To line up support would take time and energy, but it was an opportunity that excited me, and I was prepared to fight for it.

Governor Ventura's larger-than-life persona impressed me when I showed up for my interview. He had an imposing physical presence—tall, robust, with a rugged appearance—and he exhibited a strong sense of self-assurance. In a deep and gravelly voice he asked me, "What's your plan of action as the Commissioner of Corrections, Sheryl?" Before I could answer, he continued, "You understand, it's no walk in the park. You'll oversee prisons and community corrections, handle hardened criminals, and chase down those on the run. What makes you think you're the right one for this tough job?" He looked down to scan some papers, and I had a full view of his completely bald head. I tried to gather my thoughts.

"I've seen people going through the criminal justice system like it's a revolving door," I said. "Nobody tries to focus on rehabilitating those damaged lives." The Governor nodded encouragement. "I would focus on reducing recidivism by healing the brokenness of those involved in committing crimes. This would involve addressing the root causes of their criminal conduct."

"And what are those root causes?" he asked with a quizzical look.

"I think criminal behavior is driven by drugs and alcohol. Mental illness also plays a huge role, as does inadequate education and the absence of a moral compass."

The Governor's no-nonsense approach was both engaging and intimidating. He didn't shy away from speaking his mind. "How do we get to the bottom of what's causing crime? See, I'm all for giving folks a second shot, but there's gotta be some real, tangible results from our actions. We can't just talk about change; we need to see it." He cocked his head, awaiting my response.

Governor Ventura's probing questions and attentiveness made it clear we were just getting started. The smell of his ever-present cigar permeated the room and reminded me of my grandfather, a devoted public servant who would've wanted this position for me.

"I think we could reduce recidivism if we treated these causes, to encourage offenders to recover in ways that would reform their conduct and change their lives."

"Tell me more," he said.

"During the 20 years I've worked in the criminal justice system, I've seen inmates change dramatically. When people get locked up, it's a wake-up call. But simply warehousing them without providing resources for them to change doesn't help. By investing in areas such as substance abuse, higher education, and faith-based programming, we can truly heal the brokenness of many offenders."

Governor Ventura raised an eyebrow. "All right. But we need proof, not just promises." Clearly he was earnestly searching for innovative solutions to age-old problems. I could feel the stirrings of a new era—one that would shift from the traditional, punitive approach to one that emphasized positive change. His campaign had underscored his commitment to reforming the status quo, and it was evident to me he wasn't merely looking to fill positions in his Cabinet; he sought true partners to reach this goal.

Governor Ventura appointed me to the position of Minnesota Commissioner of Corrections on February 9, 1999, the first female to hold the office in its nearly 40-year history and the only person who hadn't worked in the Minnesota correctional system. When he called to ask me to serve, his words were imbued with expectations. "You'll be stepping into a ring with some tough characters, that's for sure. But here's the deal: I expect you to put in the hard yards, bring the government right back to the doorstep of the people, get into some genuine talk with the real folks out there, and most importantly, bring home results we can see and measure. That's your mission, Sheryl!"

"I'll give it all I've got, Governor. It's an honor to be part of your team, and I know we can make a difference."

Stepping into the role of managing our state's correctional system was a formidable task, especially considering the lack of knowledge of the general public and their significant apprehension about the system. My responsibilities included the management of a $400 million budget and the oversight of a workforce comprised of 3,800 employees. Also involved were overseeing several prisons and juvenile correctional facilities, licensing jails, and running community corrections programs. However, this was merely the beginning. In line with the Governor's vision of making government operations more transparent and to engage the citizenry, I formed several citizen advisory groups and recruited community leaders to serve. Each of these leaders had demonstrated success in their respective fields addressing key issues facing offenders such as education, healthcare, specific needs of female offenders, religious services within the prisons, juvenile justice, job training, mental health issues, and substance abuse. These groups were charged with evaluating the needs of the Department, suggesting ways to address them, and providing ongoing support. Most of the members had never stepped inside a prison or been part of the criminal justice system before. Yet their expertise would be invaluable to understanding the problems we sought to address, and to formulating strategies to lower the rate of reoffending. To rehabilitate the offender population and to create a correctional system that went beyond punishment toward a road to rehabilitation was our larger and ambitious goal.

One of the people I enlisted for the citizen advisory group was former Governor Al Quie, who had appointed me to the bench over 15 years before. A life-long Lutheran and one of the *National Prayer Breakfast* founders, his political and personal endeavors were guided by his deep religious faith. After his term as governor, he spent much of his time helping prisoners by encouraging them to turn to God.

I called him. "Governor, I know you've been part of Prison Fellowship for many years and that you have a deep commitment to helping offenders transform their lives. Would you consider heading up the department's advisory group on religion?"

In his mild-mannered, soft-spoken manner, Governor Quie asked, "What have you got in mind?"

"Well, I'd like a diverse group representing all faiths to come together regularly to figure out what offenders need to turn their hearts of stone into hearts of flesh."

"I like the mission, but that's a tall order. Is there anything specific you have in mind for the group?"

I explained that I hoped the citizen advisory group would investigate what has worked well in three other states that integrate faith-based programs into their prison systems to determine whether we should adopt their strategies for offenders in our state.

"Governor, do you remember when you wrote to me after my crash? You told me, 'God must, indeed, have something special for you to do.' I took those words to heart, and they motivated me to recover from my burns. Now I believe the direction I'm meant to go is to help offenders heal their fractured lives."

"Have you considered the political reality of implementing a faith-based program while Jesse Ventura is the governor?" he asked.

"An excellent point, but I believe we can do it. First, we'll research what's worked in other states. Then, we'll need to make sure that any program we consider will pass constitutional muster in a liberal state like Minnesota. Bringing legislators along with us as we conduct our due diligence will be imperative."

"What about the governor? Do you know he says that religion is for the weak-minded? He's unlikely to support this initiative, I think."

"Convincing him may be a challenge, but he's charged me with focusing on measurable results. I believe if we show him these programs work, he'll surprise us. It's worth a try. Will you please help me?"

Governor Quie agreed with one caveat. He wanted to be involved in selecting members for the group to ensure diversity by including leaders of other faiths who would represent Native American, Jewish, Buddhist, and other communities. I agreed. This was exciting and a big step forward to improve the state of the offender population.

True to his word, Governor Quie recruited a diverse group who were dedicated to the complex task of assisting the Department of Corrections to heal prisoners' lives. They met monthly, toured Minnesota's prisons, and researched the faith-based programs that were in place in Kansas, Iowa, and Texas. After several months, Governor Quie invited me to meet with the group to hear their views about starting a faith-based program in Minnesota.

With resounding support for the concept, the group was eager to move ahead. We discussed next steps and agreed that representatives from Minnesota should visit the the nation's first and most successful faith-based prison in Sugarland, Texas, to understand and perhaps replicate their work. We began the process of obtaining legal guidance to preempt any legal challenges and to ensure our program would be constitutionally viable in Minnesota. Further, we decided it would be necessary to discuss the idea with key legislators who were tasked with overseeing corrections.

Keeping these steps in mind, we pursued the program. After several months of carefully calculating each step to ensure a successful outcome, we assembled a group that would accompany me to Sugarland, Texas, including former Governor Quie, representatives from Prison Fellowship, legislators, and department representatives. We boarded a large commercial jet to Dallas. Just as I settled into my seat on the plane, anxiety caught me unaware and threatened to overwhelm me, a lingering reminder of my crash. But this time I was accompanied by a supportive group traveling with me, and we weren't flying in a small regional plane like on my first plane trip to the Mayo Clinic. My colleagues, sensing my unease, rallied around me with quiet reassurance and nudged me forward. Throughout the flight, their encouraging words reminded me of the greater purpose that had brought us together—to have an inside view of a faith-based prison. Together, we turned our focus toward the important work that lay ahead.

Our weekend in Texas was packed with meetings and observations. We engaged with corrections officials and the warden there, and discussed factors that contributed to the prison's success. We heard from volunteers from nearby churches who were committed to mentoring inmates within the prison and as they prepared for reentry into society. The highlight was interacting with the inmates themselves at Sugarland. One by one, they told us how their participation in the program had reformed them. One inmate, serving a 50-year sentence for drug-related offenses, spoke with raw honesty about how his heart, once hardened by the weight of his criminal activity, had undergone a remarkable transformation within the Texas program. "God wrecked my life," he confessed, "and I ain't been the same since."

Another prisoner who was living on Death Row shared, "This is not a program that's going to judge you or tell you what you should or are supposed to do." He spoke of the inner freedom that had been revealed to him through participation in the program—a freedom rooted not in external circumstances, but in the respect and dignity that had been instilled in him. As I listened to their stories, I was moved by the detainees' unwavering hope in a place where despair often reigns supreme. These inmates had found a light that illuminated their path toward redemption and transformation. Their stories served as a reminder of the inherent humanity that binds us all together, regardless of our past mistakes or present circumstances. The visit demonstrated the impact the prison program had on the lives of the participants. We witnessed the power it had to create meaningful change.

After our trip to Texas, the legislators who were with us indicated they were prepared to introduce faith-based programming in our state. With this backing, Governor Quie and I travelled to Washington, D.C., to meet with the founder and board chair of the national Prison Fellowship group. We discussed the feasibility of a contract with Prison Fellowship to oversee a program in Minnesota that would mirror the successful model we'd witnessed in Texas. With a green light from Prison Fellowship, my next move was to rally support from various constituent groups essential for the successful launch of the program, including the correctional workers, commonly known as prison guards. But when they, a unionized force, got wind of the concept, rebellion simmered among their ranks. They staunchly resisted any changes to the established order, fearing it could jeopardize the stability of their employment. As the first female, and outsider, to lead the Department of Corrections, I sensed their skepticism early in my role. Every time we gathered for a meeting, their voices rose over mine, subtly yet pointedly. Their opposition was even more pronounced now.

One afternoon after a particularly heated meeting, my chief deputy pulled me aside. "Commissioner, unless the correctional workers get on board, our faith-based prison proposal is likely to fail," he said. He was genuinely enthusiastic about the idea, which made his warning even more pressing.

"I'll handle it," I said. "I'll try to explain to union leadership that this initiative could reduce violence among offenders and decrease the risk to our officers. Please set up a meeting with union leadership as soon as possible."

A few days later, we scheduled a department luncheon meeting in the conference room. That morning, I could hardly button my shirt because my hands were shaking in anticipation of the meeting. What if it didn't go well? Everything rested on the response of the union leaders. If the leadership opposed our proposal, the faith-based program would certainly fail. At noon, four of us arrived for lunch—the deputy commissioner, an assistant commissioner, former Governor Quie, and myself. But nobody else had arrived. As the minutes ticked by, I grew impatient, wondering if anybody would show up. Finally, fifteen minutes later, the union president, vice-president, and treasurer wandered in. Their faces expressed caution, perhaps mixed with some curiosity, and they sat down at the opposite end of the long conference table with their arms crossed.

Attempting to diffuse the palpable tension in the air, I greeted them warmly, "Welcome, gentlemen. Thank you very much for joining us today. Please, help yourself to sandwiches, chips, and a beverage, and make yourselves comfortable while you eat. Then we can discuss the topic at hand."

Nobody moved toward the food. The importance of this meeting weighed on me. If these guys didn't get on board, the faith-based program would be dead. I gestured toward the buffet table. Taking my cue, the deputy commissioner and the assistant commissioner casually walked over to fill their plates, as a signal to others to do the same. The union leaders hesitantly followed and the atmosphere in the room gradually relaxed. We all began to eat.

Once it seemed appropriate to start the conversation, I said, "I invited you here today to discuss the faith-based program that we are considering for Minnesota. I'd like to answer your questions and listen to any concerns you might have." Their expressions remained guarded. How could I engage them? If something in the room didn't shift, all the preparation we'd done was for nothing. I continued, "Our primary concerns are for the safety of the inmates and the staff, as well as to maintain a rehabilitative environment."

When I spoke about the impressive results we'd seen at the prison in Sugarland, Texas, one of the union leaders stood up to refill his coffee cup, his movements slow and deliberate. Then with unrestrained frustration, he said, "That's all well and good, but why didn't you take anyone from the union with you on that trip?"

His comment gave me pause. I hadn't anticipated this misstep. "You're right," I said. "It was an oversight. We should have included you." I hoped my apology would allow us to continue. He nodded his head, blew on his coffee, and returned to his seat. "I'm sorry for that omission. Please be assured we want to move forward in partnership." Tension in the room began to dissipate. Encouraged, I went on, "The inmates and staff we visited talked about how the program had transformed the behaviors and attitudes of even the most hardened offenders. The entire atmosphere of the prison was unlike anything we've seen before. It was open, warm, and positive. We believe such a program could bring similar changes here."

The union president then echoed one of my foremost concerns, the very issue we had explored with the legal counsel for the Texas prison system during our visit. "What about the separation of church and state, Commissioner? How does the Texas program pass constitutional muster?"

"As an attorney myself, I share your concern." I kept my voice professional and calm. It would be hard to recover from a misstep here. "This issue, when raised in some states, has derailed the initiative." On the other side of the table, the union president cocked his head as if he didn't want to miss a word I was saying. "The constitutionality of the program hinges on its structure. State funding cannot be used to support the religious aspects of the program. We hope to find other sources of funding for those aspects. Of course, we'll need to work closely with our own legal team to ensure we steer clear of any potential issues." Their nods seemed to indicate they understood and tentatively agreed.

An intense hour-long discussion on the merits of faith-based prison programs followed. The union leaders, with raised voices, asked about how the program would impact their workloads and assignments. I assured them that correctional workers who were uncomfortable working in the program would not be required to do so, and guaranteed there would be no retribution toward anyone as a result. My assurances seemed to alleviate their fears. The meeting concluded with a plan to schedule sessions with the correctional workers themselves, to make sure we'd address the concerns of those who work directly with the inmates and to explain the proposal more thoroughly.

As the room began to clear, I turned to Governor Quie, "How do you think it went?" I asked. He paused for a moment.

"I think it was a good start. But they still have reservations about why change is needed here in Minnesota. We must garner the support of the correctional workers who'd staff the program in order to successfully launch it. Otherwise, they'll mount a campaign against us at the legislature and with the public, which will sink it." Clearly, while we'd made some headway, there was still work to be done to win over the skeptics and to ensure the program's success.

Missteps can occur in life and at home, and we weren't immune. The day before our meeting with union leaders, my son Charlie made a mistake. He and a friend had taken a deck of cards from a store at the local mall without paying for them. When the friend's mother called to tell me about it, we agreed that together we'd escort our sons back to the store to return the cards. They would confess to the clerk what they'd done and then apologize. Both boys looked like they were walking a gang plank when they approached the store. While stern with them, the clerk took the cards back, and he waited for their promise to never again take anything without paying for it.

I believe wholeheartedly in second chances, and I'd tried to teach that philosophy to my family as well. It was heartening to see them embrace the idea. I remember vividly when my sixteen-year-old daughter Sarah came to me with a problem that had occurred in school. "Mary really messed up. She got caught with beer at soccer practice and was suspended. I'm scared for her."

Mary had been Sarah's best friend since grade school.

"I understand your concern, honey," I responded. What did you say to her?"

"That everyone stumbles. This isn't the end of the world even though it may seem like it. You taught me that. What matters now is that she picks herself up and learns from her experience."

as though my children had discovered the ⟨l⟩earning from our missteps and moving forward ⟨under⟩standing. I'd tried to make the most of my ⟨life, i⟩n that moment I knew my children, and I hoped Mary, would live their lives doing the same.

I stumbled, too. My own issues within my marriage were not as easy to manage. When I became Commissioner, I noticed an unusually high rate of divorce among those working in corrections. I hoped that would never happen to me and my family. Unfortunately, for quite some time Chuck and I were drifting apart, and my marriage started to unravel after a 28-year union. My heart ached. I blamed myself. Was it the travel I did as Commissioner? Was I too immersed in my mission at the Department? Or did we grow in different directions over time? We tried to reconcile, but to no avail. Despite our best efforts, our marriage ended.

There would be a long road to getting the faith-based program off the ground. A few days after our meeting with the union folks, we moved forward. Several meetings were scheduled with the correctional workers to discuss the initiative. Initially skeptical, the participants voiced their concern over who would staff the program and how we'd ensure security. We laid out how the program wouldn't compromise prison security or burden them. When the meetings concluded, I felt they were at least open to trying the faith-based program here.

Next we had to engage with Minnesota clergy members to see if they were willing to provide mentors from their congregations. The mentors would volunteer inside the prison and also walk alongside the inmates upon their release to ensure they were welcomed and supported by churches in their respective communities. Church leaders expressed concerns about their personal safety while they'd be engaging with convicted criminals. I understood their hesitation. Drawing their attention to what the Bible says, I reminded them of the passage "whatever we can do for those in prison, we do for the Lord." The inmates coming out of our prisons would be less likely to reoffend if they had mentors to help them reenter society, I told them. The prison inmates would one day be released back to their neighborhoods, and without adequate mentoring, they would present a greater risk to society. Their response seemed promising.

The most important conversation loomed—discussing the initiative with Governor Ventura. It was crucial to have a one-on-one conversation with him, away from potential influences of his staff who might have reservations about the program. When the Governor and I were scheduled to attend the opening of a new prison sixty-nine miles from the Twin Cities, the perfect opportunity presented itself. I suggested he join me on a state plane for the trip, which provided an uninterrupted hour to discuss our proposal. I neglected to add that there wouldn't be enough seats for his staff to accompany him.

On the morning of our trip, I sat down to an early breakfast of oatmeal and blueberries. When I grabbed the newspaper, a headline screamed at me: "Governor Ventura condemns organized religion." My eyes widened in disbelief as I read about his just-published *Playboy Magazine* interview in which, among other disparaging remarks, he called religion "a crutch for the weak-minded." I choked down the rest of my breakfast. Now, everything seemed uncertain. Acutely aware the success of the faith-based initiative hinged on my ability to persuade him, the responsibility on me was tremendous. In that moment of uncertainty, I prayed, reminding myself there was no turning back. I hoped my faith would be a constant source of strength just as it had been when the engine quit in midair.

The daunting task of convincing Governor Ventura of the need for faith-based programming in Minnesota paled in comparison to my personal apprehensions. It would be my first time flying in a small aircraft since my traumatic crash. Boarding the state's six-seat, single engine Cessna would be a formidable test. I considered the pros and cons of canceling the trip five times or more between home and the airport. My mission and my faith pulled me forward, if not my refusal to let that darn airplane win. As I climbed into the passenger compartment of that tiny airplane, the flood of emotions overwhelmed me. My legs were so shaky I could hardly stand, the memory of my crash haunting every step. It was tough to breathe. I fought a vice-like tightness in my chest. I tried to reason with myself that flying is usually safe, that my crash was just a freak thing. But the fear was louder than logic and reasoning. I felt totally exposed, helpless, like a dead man walking to his execution.

Governor Ventura extended his hand to help me. I clung to him for dear life, trying to steady the violent trembling that had overtaken my body. When I slumped into the seat beside him, a wave of nausea hit me hard, leaving me lightheaded and disoriented. Gathering what little courage I had left, my voice quivered as I confessed to him, "This is my first time back in a small plane since my crash." The words barely made it out before my throat tightened in fear.

He took my hand in his, looked at me with understanding eyes, and said reassuringly, "My wife Teri is a white-knuckle flyer so I know what it's like to help someone through this. Don't worry, Sheryl, I'll do the same for you. You'll be fine, and we'll get there before you even know it."

Despite his comforting words, a sense of impending doom lingered. The engine roared to life, each vibration sending a new shockwave of terror through me. The smell in the plane, a weird mix of fuel and metal, got to me. My stomach churned, threatening to revolt, as memories of my crash surged. Flashes of that terrifying descent, the deafening roar of the engine failing as it cut in and out, the plane going down—I couldn't get them to stop. It all played in my mind like a nightmarish film on a loop. The plane started moving. Every little bump felt like a prelude to disaster. As we gained speed and the ground began to fall away, the world outside blurred and I was at the mercy of the big, uncaring sky.

The tight space of the cabin was suffocating, trapping me in my mounting panic. Governor Ventura's presence was the only thing anchoring me to reality, his occasional reassuring glances a lifeline in the storm. The plane leveled off, but the sense of crisis didn't ease. Every slight tilt or dip sent my heart into my throat, fear gripping me with cold, unyielding fingers. The shadow of the crash loomed large and menacing, tainting every moment with dread. Still, I was fiercely determined to overcome this, to take back control of my life and to face my experience head-on. These flashbacks had to stop.

Reaching 10,000 feet jogged my memory, and I recalled the job I had to do. I sat up tall, straightened my shoulders, and said a prayer to bolster my confidence, trusting that faith would guide me through this critical conversation. Notwithstanding my anxiety, the flight afforded a rare and valuable chance to have the Governor's undivided attention. There would be no better time.

I launched into the conversation with a slightly tremulous voice. "When you asked me to serve as your Commissioner of Corrections, we discussed the need to end the revolving prison door and to work toward truly healing the brokenness of offenders." He leaned toward me. A good sign. I continued, reminding him that he'd stressed getting measurable results and meaningful reform, changes that mattered.

"You asked me to involve common folks in the process of creating avenues for genuine transformation and healing."

"Go on," he said. He shifted his body position and gazed out the airplane window, distracting me for a moment, but I forced myself to stay focused and to push on.

I thought maybe I could ignore the small bouts of turbulence if I looked directly into Governor Ventura's eyes. I described the citizens advisory group on religious services I'd asked former Governor Quie to chair. I told him how this diverse group of people had met regularly to investigate how to reduce recidivism rates in our state, concluding that faith-based programs in prison were quite effective in reducing the chances of reoffending.

The Governor didn't respond. I held my breath and imagined what this program could mean for Minnesota's correctional system. Then he finally said, "All right. Let's break it down. What exactly are faith-based programs, and why are they hitting the mark so well?" Relieved by his questions, which indicated to me that he had been listening to my pitch, I saw he was trying to understand it better.

"Faith-based prison programs tap into the inmates' own personal beliefs and values and can provide them with a new perspective on life. Inmates are led to reevaluate their life choices and past actions. Deep personal transformations can occur as they develop new values and purpose. The faith-based units also offer a strong sense of community since the inmates live together, reinforcing that they are part of something bigger than themselves. This support network provides encouragement, understanding, and a sense of belonging crucial for personal growth and rehabilitation."

"Can you please be more specific?"

My words flowed as I described how these programs introduced a moral and ethical framework to guide inmates toward making better decisions. As I continued, thoughts of the crash faded. "Learning about forgiveness, responsibility, and compassion motivates inmates to change their behavior. They can develop new ways of coping with challenges and stress through prayer, meditation, or reflection, which offer a sense of hope and a chance for redemption."

"But how does this lessen the incidence of reoffending?"

At that moment, the jet jerked. I grabbed the armrest; my mouth suddenly so dry I had trouble swallowing. How could I block out the distracting sounds of the jet and the unsettling turbulence we were encountering? I inhaled deeply to calm my nerves. Perhaps I could gather my thoughts again.

"Governor, when individuals undergo profound internal changes, their external behaviors often change as well. A person who has developed new values and a moral compass is less likely to engage in criminal behavior because they have better coping strategies, they feel more responsible for their actions, and they're motivated to contribute positively to society. The support network from these programs continues on an ongoing basis to guide them after their release, reducing the likelihood that they will fall back into their old patterns."

"Okay, I get it. All this faith-based program talk sounds promising, but the real challenge? Convincing the lawmakers and the public that we're not just taking a soft approach on crime. How do you make them see this isn't about going easy? That it's about making real, tough changes from the inside out?"

I explained that we'd talked to several legislative leaders who indicated an openness to the idea. We'd also consulted community leaders who said it's high time we tried something new because what we've got now isn't working. I described we had a solid team ready to roll up their sleeves to help us make it happen.

An announcement over the intercom threw my body back into turmoil. The pilot interrupted, "We're about to land. Please make sure your seat belts are fastened."

Reassuring to some passengers, but not to me. The flight was almost over, but I had to get through the landing. Governor Ventura hadn't voiced approval or commitment to go ahead with the concept either. There might not be another chance.

"Governor," I interrupted. "Do I have your permission to proceed with the plans I've outlined?"

"It seems like you've really dug into the details on this one, and I respect that. Okay, Sheryl. So, here's the deal: I'm on board with giving it a shot. But let's be clear—this program's gotta be voluntary for the inmates. I'm not in the business of forcing religion on anyone who's not looking to jump in. If we keep it that way, count me in."

I assured him that we would proceed with caution. No one would be coerced into our faith-based program. Then the wheels touched down. A profound sense of relief washed over me. We landed safely, and my mission had been accomplished. Deeply satisfied, the Governor and I disembarked from the plane, united.

We forged ahead. The Department signed a deal with Prison Fellowship to kick off a faith-based program at one of our medium security prisons, and we instituted a series of speaking engagements in the community to lay out our plans and to recruit volunteers. The response was overwhelmingly positive. During a conversation with other department officials, I suggested we name the program after Governor Quie. In 2002, the first inmates entered the Albert H. Quie Inner-Change Freedom Initiative at the Minnesota Correctional Facility in Lino Lakes. Remarkably, ten years later, the risk of reoffending had decreased by 35 percent among the participants. Minnesota became a national model for effective faith-based programs inside the prison walls.

Healing inmates would be challenging without also addressing the issue of substance abuse within the correctional system. I hoped to tackle it. Approximately 90 percent of Minnesota's inmates are diagnosed with substance use disorders. The strong link between substance abuse and crime has been documented. Healing involves many layers—breaking free from substance abuse, addressing underlying emotional and mental issues, repairing relationships, and improving overall well-being, to name a few. I was intimately familiar with this issue. More than I wanted to be. My own brother was a recovering alcoholic. I understood how substance abuse affects entire families who are oftentimes helpless to address the problem until the chemically dependent person hits rock bottom. My brother did. He was forced to come to terms with his problem when he landed in a jail cell. Observing his more than 20 years of sobriety convinced me that we needed to do more to help the incarcerated deal with this problem.

During my tenure as Commissioner, we established the *Chemical Abuse and Recovery Evaluation (CARE)* advisory group to help individuals in Minnesota's criminal justice system overcome addiction. I called on my long-time friend, head of publishing and educational services at the Hazelden Foundation, and previously cofounder of the Institute on Black Chemical Abuse, to be our chairperson. The State of Minnesota boasted about its two preeminent chemical dependency treatment entities, the Minnesota Department of Corrections and the Hazelden Foundation, but there had been little, if any, communication or collaboration between these two major providers. Our *CARE* group changed that by bridging the gap between them. Stakeholders from both organizations, other experts, and concerned citizens came together to address the common challenge of substance abuse within the correctional system.

The Minnesota Department of Corrections and the Hazelden Foundation worked in tandem to address these complex social issues. The former helped educate Hazelden staff about the unique aspects of treating the chemically addicted in the criminal justice system, while the latter provided educational and training programs, free of charge, for Department of Corrections personnel involved in the addiction and mental health fields. The two organizations created a structured treatment curriculum known as *The New Direction* to guide prisoners, to teach them how to maintain sobriety and to conduct themselves in a pro-social, law-abiding manner. It was the first collaborative effort between the Minnesota Department of Corrections and a private agency. Bolstering parole and probation programs throughout the country, *A New Direction* has become one of the flagship curriculums used to treat criminal and addictive behavior in prisons, community corrections, and jails throughout the country.

Lastly, there was the matter of schooling for inmates. For cost-saving reasons, my predecessor had eliminated higher education opportunities for inmates. My research showed a significant reduction in recidivism rates for those prisoners who participated in prison education programs. In fact, the higher the degree, the lower the recidivism rate. Reinstating higher education inside Minnesota's prison walls was met with resistance from legislators. Why should inmates receive college education courses free of charge while their children and others incurred significant debt to pay for their education? The *Education Citizens Advisory Group*, led by the Lieutenant Governor, an educator herself, devised a creative approach to address this concern. They recommended that proceeds from inmate phone calls—which did not involve state funds—be used to fund the inmate courses. It was a great solution. Higher education was reinstituted for Minnesota prisoners, which we hoped would disrupt the cycle of negativity and hopelessness that often pervades prison life and provide a crucial step towards personal healing, social rehabilitation, and fostering a more inclusive and empathetic society.

With that, I concluded my term as Corrections Commissioner. I came to realize that my experience as a plane crash survivor and as Commissioner were linked. The journeys were both cathartic and highlighted the importance of giving people a second chance in life.

While losing the election was initially completely destabilizing, the loss eventually revealed itself to be a significant win. It redirected my path toward a role that was immensely rewarding and purposeful. Although different from what I had initially envisioned for myself, the Commissioner position provided the opportunity to make a significant impact on individual lives and the community, turning what seemed like a personal defeat at the time into a huge "win" for others and me.

I met with Chuck Colson, former White House Counsel, to promote a faith-based prison in Minnesota

Sheryl Ramstad

Minnesota's correctional delegation touring Texas faith-based prison

Notice of Commissioner appointment

Living Life Full Throttle

My family with Governor Ventura when I was announced Commissioner of Corrections

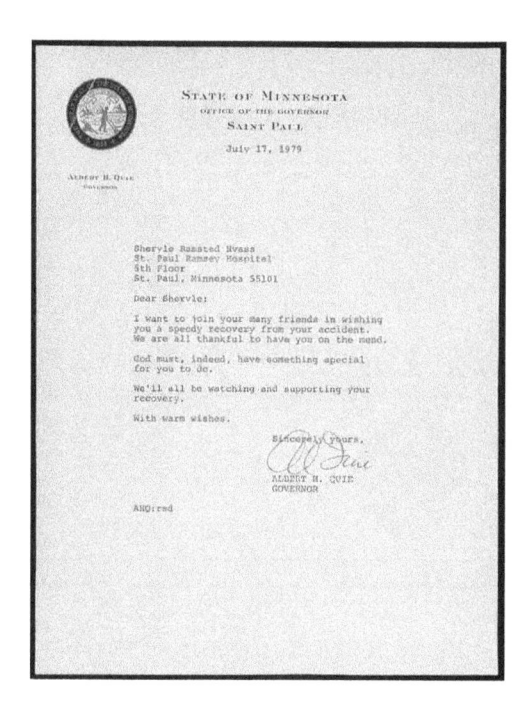

Governor Quie's letter to me while I was hospitalized

CHAPTER 9

Ain't No Mountain High Enough

The October air was crisp and tinged with the scent of fallen leaves. I made my way to the café, where Pam and I would usually meet each month. Pushing the door open, the familiar jingle of the bell greeted me, along with the comforting aroma of freshly brewed coffee. I spotted Pam at our favorite corner table, her eyes sparkling with excitement.

I'd first met Pam when our daughters began kindergarten. A vivacious woman just a few years younger than I, Pam laughed easily and her naturally curly, short reddish-brown hair perfectly matched her vibrant personality. We each had a girl and a boy, and coincidentally, they ended up in the same grades together from preschool through high school.

Watching our kids grow up side-by-side enriched the special bond we had.

I settled into the chair across from Pam and wrapped my hands around a steaming cup of coffee. Pam leaned in. "Guess what? I'm going to climb Mt. Kilimanjaro. Want to join me?" Pam and I had shared our mutual love for travel, and over the years we toured destinations as varied as the city of Paris and the mountains of Colorado. Her work had taken her all over the world, and I was always amazed at how she balanced her extensive travels with her family life. But I was taken aback, unsure where Mt. Kilimanjaro was, let alone what climbing it might entail. The thrill of an undertaking with my dear friend instantly sparked my interest. With growing curiosity, I urged her to tell me more.

"Do you know Tom Wirth? He founded *Books for Africa*."

The name sounded familiar. "We've never met. Aren't you on the board?"

Pam nodded vigorously. "Tom's 70th birthday is on February 5th, and he plans to deliver the organization's one-millionth book to Tanzania on that day at the mountaintop. Several board members are going. Are you interested?"

I took a bite of a blueberry scone and considered the proposal. I liked the idea of supporting this organization, and from what Pam had said over the years, they'd done great things by collecting books destined for landfills and sending over 50 million of them to children in Africa. I recalled the grueling training from my marathon days and hesitated. This had to be even more strenuous. "Maybe...How would you ever get in shape and train for something like that?"

"Good question. Training will be intense. It's not just any mountain—it's the highest free-standing peak in the world—19,341 feet." Pam was quite animated. "The climb's tough, no doubt, but we'll take it slow and steady. One foot in front of the other. We can totally handle it."

Her energy was infectious, and her ability to draw people into her world was working. "Over the next three months, we'll build up our endurance. Won't be long before we're hiking six to eight miles a day. It's going to be such fun." It was impossible not to get swept up in her excitement. "And we'll need to get used to the high altitudes. Breathing up there is a whole different ball game." She laughed, clearly thrilled about it, and her passion made the idea of climbing Mt. Kilimanjaro with her seem not only possible but exhilarating.

Our drinks cooled while we let our imaginations wander. Then a concern popped into my mind. The thought of being left on a mountainside without her was chilling. I fretted and had to say something. "Okay, I'll give it a try if you promise me one thing—we'll stick together on this climb. If either of us runs into trouble, we'll help the other one out. You won't leave me behind, and I won't abandon you. Deal?" Of course, what haunted me was that I could have a flashback about my crash, alone and without anyone to help me through it.

"Sheryl, we're in this together—all for one, one for all. You have my promise."

We parted ways with a plan to put together a training schedule. When I walked to my car, I imagined standing atop Mt. Kilimanjaro, witnessing the world from an extraordinary vantage point. The thought of seeing such breathtaking views thrilled me. I looked up a photo on Google and suddenly a wave of apprehension washed over me. The reality of what I'd just committed to began to sink in. The sheer magnitude of climbing not just any mountain, but the tallest free-standing peak in the world, abruptly felt overwhelming. Doubts crept in. What about leaving my family? Was I capable of such a feat? In that moment, which happened much too often, memories of my catastrophic crash came flooding back. Facing uncertainty wasn't my forte. I wanted to do the climb but couldn't help thinking of myself in the headlines again.

Before my accident, I was fearless. I wouldn't have given a second thought to traveling to an unknown country halfway across the world to tackle this climbing feat. Back then, I'd had a sense of reckless abandon, living life in all its glory, the concept of my mortality as foreign to me as the farthest star. I embraced every escapade with an "I'm game for anything" attitude. I wasn't at all concerned when performing aerobatics with a friend, and flying upside down in a single-engine plane doing rolls, loops, stall turns, and spins. Then I believed I was invincible. The notion I could become a statistic that filled the pages of newspapers and the news broadcasts never occurred to me. Of course, I was younger then, too, and didn't have a family that relied on me.

The crash changed it all. I questioned everything I'd once taken for granted. And since the newspaper headline triggered my flashback the first time I returned to the burn clinic, memories of the crash revisited me over and over. Every accident report, every tragedy that was broadcasted on TV since then, made me feel like I was reliving my own. Why did the engine suddenly quit when I was about to land? Possessed by the terror of those 20 seconds before the plane burst into flames, I was terrified I'd die and kill others nearby. And my flashbacks weren't sparked only by adventures. Whenever I entered a crowded elevator or when I latched the door to a restroom stall, the claustrophobia would set in, and I had to escape. I tried hypnosis, but that didn't rid me of my fear. For decades, I wasn't able to let go of the trauma. The emotional burdens lingered and continued to plague me.

That carefree woman who'd embarked on her first solo flight with a heart full of dreams was gone. The accomplishments I'd achieved in the years following my crash hadn't resolved these emotional burdens. Physically, I'd made significant strides; my wounds had healed, my body had regained its strength. Running marathons and succeeding professionally provided a measure of healing and a sense of achievement. But they only skimmed the surface of the deeper wounds. A more complicated reality simmered. Despite the external markers of success, my internal landscape was marred by trauma that had settled in my psyche, revealing a deeper truth: what I'd achieved—professionally, athletically, personally—were, in a sense, superficial treatment for the more profound wounds inflicted by the crash. They were merely attempts to reclaim control, like battling symptoms without curing the disease. My internal turmoil persisted, an incessant storm that refused to abate, at times, overwhelmed by crippling self-doubt and grieving the loss of the life I used to live. A pervasive fear of vulnerability whispered "caution" with every decision I made.

When the flashback eased a bit, I staggered toward a nearby bench and collapsed. Doubts swirled chaotically through my mind. I cradled my head to contain the turmoil within. My breathing grew erratic. A passerby approached, her voice cutting through the fog of my distress. "Are you okay, ma'am? Is there anything I can do for you?" Her voice pulled me back from the precipice of my own fears.

"No, thanks. I think I'll be okay."

I attempted to rise from the bench, but my knees buckled. My body shook at the thought of Mt. Kilimanjaro. What if I had a panic attack? What if there were a rockslide or I broke a bone? Even a twisted ankle could rapidly turn into a big problem without medical help up there. I couldn't help thinking that people died on that mountain. Then, my thoughts veered to my family. Putting them through the possibility that I might injure myself or maybe even die was indefensible. I sighed. I needed to try to make it to my car to get home to safety, but it was ten feet away, which seemed like a marathon.

When I finally wobbled to my car and got into the driver's seat, I propped my head on the steering wheel. Grabbing a Kleenex tucked away in my purse, I blew my nose. The force of the blow seemed to momentarily quiet the storm that raged inside me. Still shaking, I started the car and headed home. The world outside seemed to move in slow motion, and at each turn and stoplight I reflected on the shadows of my past that had irrevocably altered my life. I had to do something drastic to rid myself of the painful flashbacks.

I couldn't shake off the allure of reaching that majestic peak. I wondered if the climb might force me to engage in a way I'd never dared before. Perhaps it would strip away the layers of dread, diffidence, and doubt that had built up over time. It was a daunting prospect, but with each mile, I discerned a new chapter could be waiting, holding the promise of another crucial step in my long-term healing.

Turning into the driveway of my home, I killed the engine and snapped the radio off, leaving me in silence. A sense of resolve began to take hold. The mountain represented more than just a physical obstacle; it was a symbol of my internal struggle. Despite second thoughts, the call was too strong to ignore. Overcoming my fears and pushing beyond my perceived limits, climbing Mt. Kilimanjaro was no longer only Pam's dream; it was becoming my own.

Mt. Kilimanjaro was an environment that left no room for avoidance or denial. The harsh conditions and the sheer scale of the mountain would force me to confront head-on the vulnerabilities that had been raging within me since the crash. Healing would demand openness to delve into the deepest recesses of my psyche, to confront the darkness that resided there—pain from the physical changes to my body, anger at the engine quitting, and sadness for all that my family and I had gone through. I could no longer push these feelings aside. Climbing Kilimanjaro began to symbolize for me that I might be able to reclaim my narrative and move from being a victim to a victor. I knew it would not be easy. I had to make peace with my past and learn to live with my trauma rather than be defined by it. If I could embrace the messiness of my emotional landscape and peel back each layer of fear and denial, perhaps it would bring me closer to the core of my trauma, and I hoped, closer to complete healing. Perhaps it would prove, as they say in the song, "there ain't no mountain high enough."

I went ahead and purchased a Northwest Airlines ticket to Kilimanjaro International Airport commencing January 28, returning February 7, 2006. My training schedule, I realized, would have to be rigorous and planned carefully. With only three months before climbing Africa's highest peak, I had to build my strength, endurance, and confidence fast. Painstakingly, I mapped out weekly goals, then translated them into attainable daily efforts. I'd exercise seven days a week and include a mix of cardio and weight training, hikes, and stair climbing to ensure my knees could handle the relentless ascent and descent of the mountain. Would it be enough? I hadn't run marathons in over 15 years, and my endurance, once good, had declined.

I pushed myself to exercise on a variety of machines to increase my heart rate and my endurance—the stair stepper, leg press, elliptical machine, treadmill, and occasionally rowing machine. On alternate days, to strengthen my core and my muscles, I focused on strength training—sit-ups, push-ups, and free weights. Others might think my training unreasonable, too relentless, even bordering on the extreme. But there was no other way for me. Obsessed with the aim to climb Mt. Kilimanjaro, I wanted to reach the top in good shape, strong enough to truly savor the view and the accomplishment.

Almost sheepishly, I shared my schedule with Pam to let her know she'd be welcome to join me anytime. "That's more than I can handle," she confessed. "I'll train with you when I can, but I think I'll get ready in a more relaxed manner." I respected her choice. She knew her own limits. My way, rightly or wrongly, would be to embrace training with the same fervor I applied to all my endeavors. Preparing for Mt. Kilimanjaro was no different—living life full throttle, whatever the circumstances.

The weeks leading up to the climb were overflowing with intense training sessions. The gym became my second home. I spent hours sweating and straining under the weight of my ambition. I squeezed my training in whenever I could find the time—early mornings, late afternoons, and weekends when I wasn't on the bench, sometimes even during the lunch hour. I questioned myself—was I pushing too hard? Looking back, perhaps it was all part of an effort to prove to myself that I could achieve any goal I set my sights upon, even including climbing one of the world's tallest mountains. The physical exhaustion at the end of the day seemed like a small price to pay for the ultimate reward. Some of my guilt was assuaged since Sarah and Charlie were away at college, and Kristina spent a lot of her time with Chuck.

The IDS Center, at 57-stories, the tallest skyscraper in Minneapolis at the time, was located just a few blocks from my office. Twice a week or more, I'd don a backpack loaded with bricks to climb the stairs of this impressive building. Lifting my own body and the heavy backpack while battling gravity and fatigue mounting 1,280 steps took a monumental effort. The bricks in my backpack pulled me down with each move and mocked my efforts, the straps digging into my shoulders, leaving marks from the weight. My muscles screamed in protest, and my body ached. The constant burn in my calves, thighs, and lower back made me wonder if I was crazy. But I'd set an ambitious goal, and I didn't waver.

Preparing for the climb was also a huge test of willpower. Doubts continued to surface in my mind, threatening to derail me. Why was I doing this? What was I trying to prove? Whenever I questioned my ability to do the climb, the memory of surviving my airplane crash surfaced. It's a powerful motivator. How hard I'd fought for my life. I drew upon that same stamina to keep going. My family urged me on, assuring me that the effort would be worth it. Pushing doubts aside, I visualized myself standing on the pinnacle of Africa. I did get stronger, and my body adapted to the grueling regimen. My confidence grew to the point that Mt. Kilimanjaro was no longer a distant dream. It became a tangible goal within my reach.

One night a week, I'd join a group of fellow enthusiasts from the *Books for Africa* trip, and our training took an adventurous turn outdoors. We met in Stillwater, Minnesota, a 45-minute drive from Minneapolis, at an outdoor historic and serpentine staircase dating back to 1857 with 157 steps and ascending 115 feet. My goal was to go up and down this staircase at least four times each session. The cement steps were irregular and varied in height and depth. Their unevenness demanded a different approach from the uniform, predictable stairs of the IDS Center. Climbing in a steady, rhythmic manner wasn't possible, and we had to adapt to the characteristics of each step. But there was a scenic reward at the top, a bluff that overlooked the St. Croix River.

I suppose I was a glutton for punishment as I carried my weighted backpack here, too. The stairs seemed endless, each flight more daunting than the last. I focused on my breathing—inhale, step, exhale, step. The sound of my heavy breathing mixed with the thud of my boots hitting the steps created a rhythm that helped maintain my pace as sweat poured down my face and stung my eyes. Many times I wanted to fling off the backpack and collapse. However, every step I took with that heavy load was a step closer to scaling Mt. Kilimanjaro.

After we'd completed the strenuous climb, I'd join the group, which would convene in a cozy local coffee shop at the base of the stairs. Removing my backpack felt like I was shedding a layer of heavy armor. My body was sore, and I was exhausted, but a sense of achievement transcended my pain. We climbers had a special camaraderie. We'd discuss our upcoming trip to Africa, exchanging insights on our individual training, offering each other encouragement and advice, and we fostered a sense of shared purpose.

In early December, Pam asked me to join her on a trip to Breckenridge, Colorado. There we could acclimatize to high-altitude hiking in preparation for the trek. Twice the elevation of Denver and one of the highest towns in the Colorado Rockies, Breckenridge was the perfect setting for our training. The beauty of the landscape struck me. The snow-capped mountains and crisp, clear air were invigorating, albeit a bit daunting considering the physical challenges that lay ahead.

Like sailors navigating the uncharted waters, Pam and I plunged into the world of hiking and trail running at this high altitude. Each step involved battling the thin, elusive air with the determination of warriors. During our inaugural run, I exclaimed, "Pam, I can't catch my breath," my words punctuated with labored breathing reminiscent of a fish gasping for air on dry land. "I thought I was in good shape, but I'm so winded I can hardly stand it."

Pam mirrored my struggle. She was contorted like a pretzel, and her hands clutched her abdomen. "My heart rate is going so fast it feels like it's jumping out of my body."

Despite the challenges, we persevered and made progress. My heart rate eventually slowed to a more manageable rhythm. We doubled our water intake, a liquid lifeline in the arid climate. Beverages laced with electrolytes became our elixir, and we hoped a diet rich in calories and carbohydrates would shield against the specter of altitude sickness. With each passing day, our bodies acclimatized, resilient like trees bending in the wind. Prolonged exertion at high altitudes required not only physical stamina but also mental toughness. In moments of uncertainty, the sheer willpower that helped me survive in the past fueled my resolve. The wellspring of inner strength that had pulled me through my harrowing ordeal would push me through fatigue and discomfort to climb Mt. Kilimanjaro.

The hikes in Breckenridge also provided an opportunity to test and adjust our gear—hiking boots, backpacks, and layered clothing—to ensure they were comfortable and functional. This was especially important for the boots, which would be my primary support during the long days of trekking. I learned how to wear multiple layers of clothing that could be adjusted according to the changing weather—starting with three layers in the cool mornings, removing the mid-layer as it warmed up, and then making adjustments when we reached windy or higher altitudes. Heat would be quickly lost when our extremities and our heads were exposed so we added hats, gloves, and scarves to regulate our body temperature. At the end of the week, I felt better prepared for and more confident about the climb ahead.

Before I knew it, January 28th had crept up on us. Pam and I took a cab to the Minneapolis-St. Paul International Airport to embark on our much-anticipated adventure to Kilimanjaro. The first eight-hour flight took us to Amsterdam. We'd left Minneapolis in the evening with the intention of sleeping on the way, but we were too excited to sleep. After a brief layover in Amsterdam to stretch our legs, we boarded the 10-hour flight to Kilimanjaro International Airport, and on that flight we managed to get a little sleep. The previous wakeful night had caught up to us.

After collecting our luggage at the Kilimanjaro airport, we took a 45-minute taxi ride to Mountain Village to wait for the rest of our trekking crew to join us. Pam and I had intentionally arrived a day before everyone else to acclimatize to the elevation and to rest after the long flight. Mountain Village, we discovered, was enchanting. Individual thatch-roofed huts served as hotel rooms. A bellman carried the bags to our hut, taking us into another world. The sounds of nature, the sight of monkeys swinging playfully among tree branches, and the rustic charm of our thatch-roofed hut were already unforgettable.

That night, I slept deeply, comforted by the quiet of the plantation, excited about the days ahead. I woke up refreshed the next morning, eager to explore. We stopped at the market in Arusha where we immersed ourselves in the local culture and the hustle and bustle of market life. The colors, scents, and sounds converged to create a sensory overload that seemed quintessentially African. The kaleidoscope of colors struck me. Stalls adorned with goods of every hue imaginable were a feast for the eyes. Brightly colored fabrics stacked high featured intricate patterns and designs, indicative of the local Maasai culture and other Tanzanian traditions. And the aroma of spices filled the air: a hardy mix of cinnamon, cardamom, cloves, and nutmeg displayed in heaps and baskets, enticing customers with their exotic scents. Nearby, vendors sold fresh fruit and vegetables in stalls overflowing with tropical produce—mangoes, bananas, avocados, and pineapples, alongside local varieties of maize, beans, and leafy greens. A contrast to what I was used to back home, in the meat section of the market butchers displayed their cuts in the open air, everything from beef and goat to chicken. The market's no-frills approach to meat selling was shocking but an authentic glimpse into the local way of life.

Live animals were also part of this scene. Chickens clucked. Goats and sometimes cattle were tied near the meat section, and it was not uncommon to see stray dogs navigating through the crowd or cats lounging in a quieter corner of the market. Teeming with people, the market attracted locals bargaining for the best prices, and vendors called out to attract customers and visitors like myself. People moved in a rhythmic flow, negotiating prices, exchanging money, and carrying goods in woven baskets atop their heads.

My most vivid memory of the village market was seeing a young African man wearing an orange T-shirt with the words "Ramstad Team" emblazoned in bold black letters across his front. It was my brother's campaign T-shirt, a distinctive and familiar item from back home in Minnesota. I was astonished to see it in such an unexpected place. Without thinking, I reached for my camera to capture a photo to send back to my brother. I couldn't help myself. I cried out, "That's my brother's T-shirt!" The words came out louder than I intended, echoing through the noises of the market.

The T-shirt wearing man was bewildered. He obviously couldn't understand what I'd said, and my sudden outburst only added to his confusion. I looked around, hoping to find someone who could translate to bridge the gap between us. Then our eyes met. The man turned around and bolted with fear in his hurried steps. Perhaps he thought I was accusing him of theft and would escalate the situation by involving the police over the shirt he was wearing?

Without thinking, I sprinted after him, hoping to explain and to ask for his permission to take a photo. I could see his eyes widening in surprise and confusion. Raising my hands in a gesture of peace, I slowed down trying to convey that I meant no harm. "I'm so sorry," I said, breathless from the chase. "It's just that your T-shirt is from my brother's political campaign back in Minnesota. I never expected to see it here, in Tanzania. Could I please take a picture of you wearing it?" I stood there feeling the intensity of the man's stare, his confusion. Of course, he still couldn't grasp what I was saying, and I was ashamed for my insensitive behavior. I left quickly.

Later, when I had a second to think about it, I realized the shirt was likely from a shipment of used clothing from the United States. I was embarrassed that I hadn't handled the situation with more finesse. I failed to show him the respect he deserved. In his eyes, I must've appeared like the epitome of the "ugly American"—brash, inconsiderate, and insensitive. My thoughtlessness had caused a disturbance and also had frightened him, which troubled me greatly.

After the fiasco, Pam and I spent the rest of the day as tourists, drifting from place to place exploring the town of Arusha. Surrounded by lush greenery and stunning landscapes, the roads were lined with small shops and businesses, which ranged from local eateries serving traditional Tanzanian dishes to huts with goods and textiles. The air was filled with the sounds of Swahili music and the chatter of locals. During our walk through the vibrant village, we saw the fusion of the traditional and modern, the blend of rural charm and urban energy, and the melding of local customs with global influences.

That evening, we selected a charming and authentic establishment for dinner that radiated the warm spirit of East African hospitality. Nestled in the heart of the city, it had a modest façade with a vibrant, hand-painted signboard welcoming patrons. The interior had a rustic charm, and the walls were adorned with traditional Tanzanian arts and crafts, including colorful batik fabrics and intricate beadwork. The servers, dressed in traditional attire, added to the authentic atmosphere of the place. We were greeted by the inviting aroma of spices and grilled meats.

Dinner began with 'ugali', a Tanzanian staple made from maize flour. It had a thick, dough-like consistency and a subtly sweet taste. I also enjoyed 'nyama choma': goat marinated in a blend of local spices and grilled to a smoky and tender flavor. Complimenting the meat was 'mcicha,' a dish made from fresh, leafy greens, like spinach, cooked with tomatoes, onions, and a hint of coconut milk. We sampled 'pilau', a fragrant rice dish cooked with spices like cumin, cardamom, and cloves, mixed with pieces of chicken and vegetables. The meal was accompanied by 'kachumbari,' a fresh salad made with tomatoes, onions, and chili, seasoned with lemon juice and salt. To end the meal, we drank a cup of 'chai masala,' a spiced tea with hints of ginger, cardamom, and cinnamon. As an American trying Tanzanian cuisine for the first time, I was impressed with the diversity of flavors and the heartiness of the dishes.

After dinner, we returned to our hut in Mountain Village. Although I was utterly exhausted, I still took time to jot down thoughts in my diary, a ritual that brought me both comfort and clarity. My mind wandered to our fellow *Books for Africa* hikers joining us the following day. I wasn't acquainted with any of them before signing up for the trek. I wondered what kind of conversations we would have and the bonds we would form as ambassadors of hope, motivated by our desire to bring books to remote areas of Africa and the belief that every child deserved the right to read and learn.

The soft hum of the night enveloped me as I lay in bed. I finally let the weariness of the day take over. Dreams of dusty trails, laughter-filled campsites, and backpacks filled with our daily necessities danced in my mind, soothing my restless spirit. In my heart, I knew I was ready for this trek.

Our *Books for Africa* group arrived the next morning. After finishing breakfast, we all took an 80-minute taxi ride from Arusha to the southeast entrance of Kilimanjaro National Park, known as the Marangu Gate. There, the 69-year-old founder, Tom Wirth, paid our park entrance fees and registered with the Parks Authority for our five-day hike on the

Marangu Route, the oldest and most popular trail to Mt. Kilimanjaro. But the route has its pros and cons. It has the highest failure rate of the seven routes because even though it is the shortest trek up the mountain, it doesn't give much time to acclimatize to the altitude: however, it's the only trail with overnight stays in dormitory-style shelters instead of tents. The three dormitories have **60-100** bunk beds equipped with simple mattresses and pillows. Often called the "Coca-Cola route," trekkers who stay there are able to purchase creature comforts such as candy bars, bottled water, and sodas.

One of the guides for our team, Desmond, had first climbed Kilimanjaro when he was fourteen. Now at sixty, he knew what to expect. He began by telling us that Mt. Kilimanjaro is higher than more than 29 Eiffel Towers stacked on top of each other. Desmond described the various climatic zones we would traverse, starting with the rainforest at the base, ascending through the moorland, and eventually climbing through the alpine desert before reaching the arctic conditions at the top. He then delved into the physical challenges—at least half of the climbers, he said, suffer symptoms of altitude sickness. This certainly gave me pause. I might have underestimated the impact of altitude that we were venturing into, an environment where our bodies would be under significant stress. My dread returned with a vengeance, and my mind raced. What if I had a panic attack on the mountainside? Would anyone be able to help me? Would the altitude bring flashbacks of my plane crash? What hadn't I considered that could happen up there? Plagued by indecision, and halfway across the world, there was no turning back; it was too late for that. I prayed that I could face my fears and attempted to talk myself through them. Then each of us grabbed our walking sticks, and at 12:45 p.m., we headed out for our first day's climb. I stared at the majestic mountain, then closing my eyes, I inhaled deeply and took the first step.

Day 1 of our hike we walked through a living, breathing greenhouse with warm and humid conditions reminiscent of a sauna. The thick canopy above us provided a respite from the sporadic drizzle. Occasionally we saw glimpses of monkeys swinging among the branches. The well-trodden route was muddy and slippery, but not overly steep, a good introduction to the trek. Sounds of chirping birds, rustling leaves, and distant waterfalls added to the lure of this tropical paradise. We climbed a total of 2,756 vertical feet over approximately five miles before reaching the Mandara Huts Camp, a collection of wooden A-frame huts nestled amidst the forest. Desmond had predicted it would take us between three and four hours, but it took us five because of our slow pace. The atmosphere at the hut was vibrant. Before dinner, while hikers from around the world shared their stories, we were served tea, hot chocolate, and popcorn. That night, I fell asleep about 9:00 pm to the sound of the forest. I'd taken the diuretic Diamox to prevent altitude sickness, as a precaution, and had to get up every two hours to go to the bathroom.

After breakfast the second day at about 8:00 am, we left the Mandara Huts Camp for the seven-and-a half-mile climb up 4,000 vertical feet to our next destination, Horombo Hut. Mist and clouds shrouded the vast open landscapes and created a mysterious, ethereal quality like being in San Francisco on a foggy day. The vegetation was sparse, but a blanket of heather created a striking contrast against the rocky terrain. The rainfall was less frequent than our first day, but when it did rain, the swift and sharp downpours felt like sudden bursts from water balloons.

A few hours into the steep hike, my boot slipped on some loose rock. Glancing downward, I saw a sheer drop into a vast unforgiving chasm. Terror surged through me. It resembled the dread I experienced when the plane's engine failed mid-flight. Teetering on the edge of catastrophe, my heart hammered against my ribs while I frantically sought stable footing. But every attempt I made only sent more stones cascading down the slope. I couldn't catch my breath. Adrenaline amplified every sound—the skittering of loose stones beneath me, my labored breathing, the distant call of a bird oblivious to my plight. Seconds felt like minutes. Grasping for survival, my mind racing, I focused every ounce of energy on finding a path to safety to avoid facing a terrifying descent.

The incident with the engine had taught me a critical lesson: overcome fear with action. Transform panic into a series of deliberate and life-saving maneuvers. Confronted by the mountain's peril, that same instinct kicked in. For a split second, the fear paralyzed me, but then, clarity won out. Memories of regaining control in the cockpit flooded back—

how concentrating on the landing, not the potential crash, had been my salvation. Clinging to this recollection, I shifted my focus from the paralyzing fear of falling to strategies for halting it. Each measured step helped me claw back control. At last, I stopped sliding, and I managed to stand firmly on the mountain again. I'd steadied myself, the danger momentarily abated, but the ghost of panic lingered. My heart still raced, and my limbs shook with both residual adrenaline and the release of tension. The mountainside, a place of beauty, had transformed into a vivid reminder of my vulnerability and the fine line between survival and calamity.

Out of my comfort zone, I wondered what else would I face? Regardless of my fear, I had to continue up the mountain. There was no other place to go. I knew I had to regain trust in myself and continue to climb. *Desiderata*, a 1927 poem by American author Max Ehrmann, came to me. My mother had given me a framed copy from her childhood, and it hung on my bedroom wall as I grew up: "Nurture strength of spirit to shield you in sudden misfortune. But do not distress yourself with dark imaginings. Many fears are born of fatigue and loneliness." I felt confident God would protect me in the event of misfortune. He'd been my co-pilot on my solo flight and he'd be with me the remainder of my ascent.

The initial shock wore off as I proceeded slowly and carefully, continuing the trek two more hours until we reached our Horombo Hut destination that afternoon. The surrounding landscape offered a view of the vast, undulating plains of the African savannah stretching out into the distance, gradually giving way to the dense, verdant rainforests that cloak Kilimanjaro's lower slopes. Gazing up at Mawenzi Peak, the crisp thin air filled with the scent of wild alpine flora, the sound of the wind whispered through the valleys and ridges. My spirit was renewed at the sight of the enduring elegance of Mawenzi Peak, an ancient volcanic cone with sharp, spire-like rocks piercing the sky.

We were able to acclimatize on the third day at Horombo Hut, one of the main rest stops for climbers on the Marangu Route. Spending time at an altitude of over 12,000 feet above sea level gave our bodies a "trial run" in a low-oxygen environment. It stimulated necessary physiological adaptations the body needs to produce more red blood cells, to enhance its ability to transport oxygen to various tissues. The day of rest also gave me a chance to recharge and to bolster my confidence in preparation for the strenuous trek ahead. Attempting to put behind me my treacherous near-fall the day before, I decided to explore the surrounding area and to admire the unique flora.

Our trek on the fourth day from Horombo to Kibo Hut, approximately six miles, had an elevation gain of approximately 3,314 feet. In the alpine desert zone, the landscape was different from the previous lush terrains we'd encountered. Vegetation was scarce, and the landscape, dominated by rocks and gravel, painted an almost otherworldly scene. At one point, my footing gave way again on the steep slopes, threatening to send me tumbling into the ominous abyss below. "Help me, I'm falling!" I yelled. My porter, thank goodness, extended his hand and I grasped it. I held on tightly as we climbed together, each step demanding more effort than the one before. I couldn't stop thinking about the possibility of twisting an ankle or breaking a bone on this, the most demanding stretch yet. The dance with danger required precision and focus, as we climbed from the height of 12,205 feet to 14,400 feet. And we still had another 5,000 vertical feet to climb ahead.

Lunchtime arrived when we weren't even halfway to our destination that day. We found a massive rock on the trail that offered a comfortable perch, and eagerly I unpacked the food we'd prepared. Pam chose a separate rock about ten feet from mine. I couldn't help noticing her sluggish movements, and she wasn't eating. Concerned, I called out to her, "Pam, aren't you going to eat something? We've got an afternoon of hiking ahead of us."

Her response was disheartening. "I'm not hungry. I just want to sleep." Her voice sounded weary, her words were slurred, and she looked visibly exhausted. Alarming. My apprehension increased as I watched her trudge toward a cave-like recess on the mountainside where she laid down on the ground.

I rushed over, knelt by her side, and shook her shoulder. "Pam? Pam? You can't lie down here. It's not safe."

"I'll be okay. Just let me rest."

I recognized her symptoms. Pam was suffering from altitude sickness, and it was critical to get her to a lower elevation immediately. "Pam," I said, my voice firm and unwavering. "Listen to me. You need to get more oxygen. If you fall asleep at this altitude, you may never wake up."

"Really, I'm okay," Pam stubbornly insisted and mumbled something like, "You go on." She began to doze off.

"Pam, you're falling asleep. We must get you down so you can breathe better."

Pam, I realized, was in serious trouble. I thought about the importance of this trek to her. Although I could hardly bear to think of Pam being unable to complete the hike, we had to face the grim reality. Descending the mountain was the only viable solution. But she remained adamant. She wouldn't or couldn't move. "Look at me," I said. "We made a promise to each other before starting this trek. We agreed to watch out for one another. I'm honoring our commitment. Pam, listen. You need to get to a lower altitude where there is more oxygen so you can think clearly." Then Pam's weary gaze met mine. My words, or perhaps the authoritative tone in my voice, seemed to penetrate the haze of her fatigue. Thank God. With a slow, albeit reluctant, nod, she conceded.

I shouted to her porter. "My friend needs your help. Come quickly. Get her to a lower altitude." The porter instantly and gently lifted Pam's arm over his shoulders and readied for the descent.

Pam was draped over her porter, and I could see her condition rapidly deteriorating. No longer able to walk, her legs failing her, she began to vomit uncontrollably. The porter lifted and carried her limp body down the rugged terrain. I felt completely helpless and afraid. I'd never forgive myself if something happened to her. She'd be alone. Should I risk going down with the porter? I knew the path wasn't wide enough for me to safely accompany them and would be dangerous for all of us.

What would she have done in my place? Did our pact to stick together mean that I should forsake my own aspirations after enduring four grueling days of ascent? My goal was within reach, merely a day's climb away. The idea of continuing without Pam was daunting. Pam, if she had been able to think clearly, would have encouraged me to complete the climb. I decided to proceed and to carry her hopes and mine with me.

I was alone again, like on my solo flight that changed the trajectory of my life. It wasn't her fault, but I felt like we'd deserted each other. It was as if I was walking into the same situation and taking another risk with no place to turn for help. I paused to look out over the vast expanse and noticed something magical. The soaring glacier-covered white mountains ran the length of the horizon like knife points pressed high and into a cloudless, cornflower blue sky. Then there appeared a glimmer of sunlight. In that moment I knew I wasn't alone in the plane, and I wouldn't be alone now. Just as God had been my co-pilot, He would be with me for the remainder of the climb. My body trembled with emotion as I whispered a prayer. I ventured higher into the alpine desert, entrusting both my own and Pam's well-being to a higher power. Each labored breath and aching muscle would be for me a symbolic ascent from the depths of despair to the pinnacle of the human spirit.

When I finally reached Kibo Hut, the landscape appeared almost extraterrestrial. In the alpine desert, at an altitude of almost 15,500 feet, the environment around the hut was stark, with a minimalistic beauty characterized by rocky terrain and a scarcity of vegetation. The desert, a barren vista, resembled the surface of the moon, and the view of the majestic snow-capped Kilimanjaro was heavenly. In the daylight, I looked down upon a sea of clouds, underscoring the altitude we'd climbed.

The physical toll of the six-mile trek that day was immense. My body ached with every movement, but the emotional fatigue proved more challenging. The weight of loneliness and exhaustion bore down on me like never before. The shared dream that had fueled the journey to this point was replaced by concern for Pam's well-being. She'd been my constant companion on this months-long journey, and the hut, a beacon of rest, offered shelter, but not the comfort of camaraderie. Lying down to rest, I tried not to be overcome with worry so I could complete what we had started together, to push forward for both of us.

The fifth day of the climb was what we'd been waiting for—to finally reach the peak. After eating, I donned my headlamp and put on layers of clothes—long underwear first, then a turtleneck, a heavy sweater, a down jacket, a scarf, a wool stocking cap, a face mask, and lined leather mittens—before heading out to find my place among our group. The trail loomed, an insurmountable wall. In the pitch dark at midnight in zero-degree weather, we began our ascent, guided by the beams of our headlights and the starlit sky lighting our way. There were groups far ahead of us winding their way up to the top so we had the benefit of following their headlights. Imagine climbing a never-ending staircase without handrails. Every step a Herculean effort, I scaled the vertical cliff with nothing but sheer willpower as my rope. The biting cold seeped through my layers of clothing and numbed my fingers and toes. I pushed onward, hoping that someone in the line ahead of me would pause so that I could rest. But they just kept going. I didn't want to think that I was climbing a mountain that was nearly 63.4 times taller than the Statue of Liberty. I focused on taking one step at a time and prayed that the Lord would help me make it to the top.

On the ascent, having learned the hard way, I placed my feet cautiously to avoid slipping on the loose volcanic scree underfoot. Without my companion by my side, each footfall echoed in silence so profound it felt as if I was moving through a vacuum, like I was breathing through a straw, the rarified air a suffocating reminder of the merciless grip of the altitude.

Our headlamps pierced through the darkness of early morning, solitary beacons in a vast ocean of blackness. The steep and rocky trail was covered with loose gravel, and I wondered if it was as treacherous as walking on a tightrope suspended over a canyon. The altitude began taking its toll. The thinning air made it even tougher to breathe. I paused frequently, whispering, "God, please help me with this challenge." Gilman's Point would mark the mountain's most challenging section. I concentrated on getting there. A checkpoint for climbers on their way to the summit at Uhuru Peak, Gilman's Point was a milestone. Uhuru Peak would still be over 600 vertical feet and more than two hours beyond. Situated at an awe-inspiring elevation of **18,885** feet near Gilman's Peak, the first light of dawn began to break through the darkness, the sun painting the sky in breathtaking hues of pink and orange like the awakening of a sleeping giant.

Bone-tired yet exhilarated, I stepped onto the icy glaciers near Gilman's Point, overwhelmed at the beauty surrounding me. The stunning glaciers, with their pristine and transcendental glow, stood in stark contrast to the warm colors of the dawn sky. Below, the vast African plains stretched out on the horizon, a tapestry of natural beauty that spoke of the grandeur of God's creation. The sun rose higher, its rays casting a golden light over the landscape and highlighting the rugged contours of the mountain. The sheer scale and beauty of the scene exemplified the incredible power and dignity of nature. Overcome by emotion as I witnessed the splendor and grandeur that God had bestowed upon our world, I thought this is where I am meant to be.

We spent about 20 minutes at Gilman's Peak taking photos, then set out on our two-hour climb to Uhuru Peak, the highest point of Mt. Kilimanjaro and the "roof of Africa." Despite the short distance, .93 miles from Gilman's Peak, the high altitude made this section of the climb exceedingly strenuous. Whenever my confidence wavered, I steeled myself with sheer willpower.

When the final stretch of the climb was upon me, my surroundings shrank into a narrow corridor of ice, rock, and sky. Each step over the rugged landscape was a battle. I had to stop frequently to catch my breath, and my lungs strained for oxygen, each shallow inhalation insufficient. My head throbbed with a persistent, dull headache while waves of nausea washed over me and every muscle ached. It was almost impossible to think. Disoriented and losing my stamina, I forced myself to drink water and consume energy bars even though my appetite was nonexistent, while uncertainty whispered in my mind.

In the vastness of the surroundings, I felt small and vulnerable. Although I had fellow climbers with me, I was alone in my struggle against the mountain. The steep drop-offs beside the narrow trail would make anyone anxious, but in my condition they terrified me. Uhuru Peak seemed to play a cruel trick, appearing deceptively close yet remaining stubbornly distant. It was difficult to push away thoughts of giving up. My prayers became a lifeline connecting me to something greater than myself, as I inched closer to my goal.

After what seemed like a void of time, I made it to Uhuru Peak. Reaching the top of Mt. Kilimanjaro was akin to breaking through a barrier of invisible forces. The sign that marked the summit stood before me, a simple wooden board, but at that moment it was the most significant object in the world. I had not only conquered the mountain, I'd dominated my own fear and doubts, and my physical and emotional limitations. The triumphant moment symbolized the distance I'd traveled from the catastrophic airplane crash to standing atop Kilimanjaro—from survival to revival.

The world spread out beneath me—a magnificent, unending mosaic. From the summit to the panoramic views, the serene beauty induced me to reflect on the fragility of life and the divine intervention that pulled me from the depths of despair to these awe-inspiring heights. The journey up Kilimanjaro was a symbolic ascent from my lowest valleys to the highest peak I could imagine. Throwing my arms in the air, I shouted with all the breath I could muster, "I made it!" The sound echoed, mingling with the wind. What a rush of exhilaration overcame me. I felt liberated, as if my spirit had been unshackled and returned to the innocence and wonder of my youth. In that moment, I had a profound revelation of what it means to be truly alive, and to stand atop the world.

I remembered that the treacherous descent awaited me. The Marangu Route, which I'd just taken up the mountain, is the path back down. We were warned by the guide to spend only a few moments on Uhuru Peak due to the extreme cold and very thin air. Our group hurried to take photos of our monumental feat, enhanced by Tom's presentation of the one-millionth book to Tanzania. The guide urged us again to head down the mountain. My spirit could not be dampened. The metaphor this experience exemplified struck me suddenly. Before every peak there must be a valley, and before moments of triumph we encounter many challenges. All of it is part of a life well lived. Preparing to leave the summit, my heart was buoyed at having reached the top and discovering a newfound energy to take back my life.

The initial part of the descent was steep and covered in loose stones. I slid down the scree, a technique that involved sliding down the gravelly slope on my boots with controlled, skiing-like movements. Exhilarating and unnerving, each slide carried a risk of losing my balance and as we made our way down the mountain, the effects of the high altitude became more pronounced. My head throbbed, and nausea washed over me. Despite these discomforts, my spirit was uplifted by the thought of reaching lower altitudes and fresh oxygen.

My mind started playing tricks on me as I skied through the barren alpine desert and traversed the upper reaches of the moorland zone. I blinked hard, trying to clear my vision. There ahead, I swore I saw a group of monkeys swinging from the branches of a tree nearby. I ducked to avoid hitting the low branches. But I knew there were neither trees nor monkeys at this altitude. Further down the route, the hallucinations grew more bizarre. I noticed colorful birds that seemed to flutter then vanish as I got closer. There were moments when I thought I saw large cats and leopards, lurking in the shadows. Each time, I had to remind myself that these were figments of my imagination, pranks played by my oxygen-deprived brain. I wondered how Pam was doing and if she'd recovered from this weird and awful feeling.

Slowly the mirages faded. The air became richer in oxygen, and my symptoms of altitude sickness lessened. The landscape transformed, and the trees became lush and the air warmer. By the time I reached lower camp, my hallucinations had stopped entirely, and I was left with a sense of relief and wonder at the strange and unexpected journey my mind had taken. The descent from Kilimanjaro, from the heights of the mountain, returned me to reality and the familiar world.

Once I'd safely returned to camp, I looked anxiously for Pam to make sure she was safe. I found her in the hut where the refreshments were located. Her face lit up when she saw me, and we rushed to embrace. "You likely saved my life up there," she said. I could see relief in her eyes and understanding, too, of the critical situation she'd been in. Pam admitted how she'd underestimated the severity of her altitude sickness—a sobering moment for both of us. The danger she'd been in and the potential consequences had she not descended reminded us of the fine line between life and death in the unforgiving wilderness. In the end, we reminisced about how we'd tested our bodies and minds in ways we'd never imagined, a fitting conclusion to an extraordinary adventure.

During my flight back to Minnesota, my thoughts wandered back to Mt. Kilimanjaro, which loomed large in my mind's eye. Climbing that monumental peak had been an endeavor like no other, challenging me to the very core of my being. Before undertaking this trek, the world around me was a minefield of triggers. The slightest sight, sound, or even a headline could catapult me back to those moments of sheer terror, unleashing a storm of memories that would haunt me without mercy. I had embarked on the climb as a pilgrimage and a release from the bondage of wounds unseen but still deeply felt.

Seeking to exorcise the flashbacks, the climb up Kilimanjaro marked a pivotal change. It didn't miraculously cure me of my trauma or purge the terrifying flashbacks, but it did something as profound. The triggers that once had the power to send me spiraling downward were now muted, their edges blunted. As I made my way up the mountain, I learned to trust myself again. The climb instilled confidence in my ability to take care of myself, to move forward regardless of the obstacles that stood in my path. Confronting my fears on Kilimanjaro finally dulled their power over me. The mountain, with its unforgiving terrain, gave me something invaluable: the strength to live with my past and to truly release me from my demons. It provided me with a new perspective and a sense of empowerment that came from overcoming what I'd once believed to be insurmountable. I reached the summit of Kilimanjaro, both in a literal and metaphorical sense.

The emotional and physical scars redefined became badges of courage and perseverance even in my own mind. I felt a deeper connection to the world and an overwhelming gratitude for the second chance at life. New chapters, though born from ashes of the old, held promise to be as rich and fulfilling as the ones I'd navigated with such careless ease. The future was mine to shape. Climbing Kilimanjaro had demonstrated that although the shadows of my past might always linger, they no longer had dominion over my spirit because at last I could see, like the song says, "there ain't no mountain high enough."

Reaching Kilimanjaro top after 4-day trek

Trekking up Mt. Kilimanjaro

Sunrise while on Mt. Kilimanjaro

CHAPTER 10

Giving Back

There are no cures for Alzheimer's. Mom's disease was progressing fast. She'd become increasingly withdrawn, never discussing her condition or how she was coping with her diminished memory. As she gradually became a shadow of her former self, I navigated the tumultuous journey of losing her and attempted to focus on acceptance. I often visited a nearby church where I'd sit alone in silence, praying for strength to accept Mom's debilitating disease.

Eventually, Mom's life slowed to a grinding halt. Compounded by two strokes, Mom finally succumbed to Alzheimer's disease. It was a complex day filled with a tapestry of emotions. My deep sense of loss was eased by knowing that she had been released from the shackles of the cruel disease.

I found peace in believing that now she was in a better place, a place where we would one day reunite.

After serving four years in the Governor's cabinet, I returned to the bench and immersed myself in various cases assigned to me. In the meantime, my insights into the healthcare system had grown, and the lessons I learned caring for my mother ignited a desire to help patients and their families during their health journeys. I was acutely aware of the significant impact visits from others with similar injuries had in supporting my family and me during my healing process. As a burn survivor, I took additional training to serve as a burn survivor peer support representative, so I could assist burn patients, interact with their families, and offer encouragement and support. These experiences inspired me to consider entering the nursing field. Becoming a burn nurse would offer me the opportunity to work directly at the bedside of burn patients during their darkest times. I was in the unique position to remind them that there is indeed life after burns.

I learned there was a master's degree program at the University of Minnesota, designed specifically for those pursuing nursing as a second career. In 2008, by then in my late fifties and having been out of the academic world for more than three decades, I decided to approach this new path cautiously by enrolling in online prerequisite classes to help me gauge my readiness for such a significant change. While juggling my full-time position as a judge, I could manage one class per semester only. My confidence increased as I completed each course.

After four years, I finished the required prerequisites and applied for the Master of Nursing program. Nothing surprised me more than receiving my acceptance letter. This spurred me to make a bold decision—to resign my judgeship. Nervous about the reaction from friends and family who I thought might try to discourage me from stepping down, I didn't disclose my reason for resigning. I thought if more people knew, I would feel greater pressure about returning to school. My desire to give back to burn patients and to contribute to their healing and care drove me to embark on this new phase of life as a full-time student. True, it was a leap of faith, but also a commitment to a personal calling that may have defied common sense but marked a new chapter in my life.

My first day of class, I felt excited and apprehensive. Even finding my way to the classroom was a challenge. After asking several people in the hallways for directions, I finally made it to a seat in the front row of the auditorium. Our instructor stood before us and smiling warmly she said, "Welcome everyone!" When the room quieted down, she continued, "I want to start by saying how exceptional you all are. We accepted only 64 of you from an applicant pool seven times that size so you truly are among a select minority chosen for the Master of Nursing program." She paused to let her words sink in. I smiled at my classmate sitting next to me, already feeling a sense of camaraderie. "In just 16 months from now, you'll have completed the program and you'll be ready to take the licensure exam to become registered nurses.

I have no doubt each of you will rise to the challenge." There was unwavering resolve within the classroom.

The instructor continued, "I'm curious about your future ambitions. I would like to see a show of hands: how many of you intend to pursue your doctorate in nursing practice after completing your master's?" The question seemed to shift the energy of the room. I looked around as hands shot up around me. To my surprise, all but five of my peers raised their hands, but I didn't raise mine. The very thought of another three years of school after finishing the master's program seemed daunting. I'd be 65 years old by then. I thought about everything I'd accomplished before getting to this point—during the last four years, while working full time, I'd taken twelve prerequisite courses that involved tests, online discussion groups, and even dissecting a fetal pig on my dining room table. Navigating the online application process had been such an ordeal that it almost deterred me from applying for the Master of Nursing program. The thought of enrolling in a doctoral program was the furthest thing from my mind. My focus was the Master of Nursing, and I would see it through, leaving others to pursue the doctorate who had more years ahead of them, and the ambition and stamina for it.

The lull of over 35 years since I'd been a student meant there would be a steep learning curve, especially to learn the new digital landscape. In law school, we didn't use computers, let alone engage with the intricacies of digital learning platforms. Submitting assignments through online drop boxes and participating in virtual discussion groups were entirely foreign to me. Had it not been for some younger people in my cohort who gave me a crash course in computer basics, I wouldn't have made it. In addition to technological hurdles, there was a formidable array of courses I had to tackle. Not just any courses, but subjects that delved into the complexities of the human body, such as anatomy, physiology, and pharmacology. Each course demanded time and a willingness to fully immerse myself in new and oftentimes complex materials. Nursing involved a completely different vocabulary and writing style than I'd used during my more than three decades in the legal profession. I was truly starting over.

When I met my cohort, it didn't take me long to see that I stood out. I was, of course, the oldest student, surpassing my peers by at least two decades. Additionally, I hadn't accumulated years of experience at the bedside like many of my classmates who'd previously worked in health-related areas. While my colleagues often referred to their clinical experiences during classroom discussions, I drew upon my personal history of hospitalizations and surgeries following my airplane crash. I wondered how my views—steeped in personal pain and recovery—resonated with my classmates who had a more traditional view of healthcare. I hoped my perspective offered unique insights.

One day when others in the class had already left, my instructor said to me, "You have such rich wisdom, Sheryl. Your opinions during class and online discussions add such important viewpoints. Please continue to share them." Her validation lifted my spirits.

The comment helped me realize that even without traditional bedside nursing, I could use my personal journey to educate and empower future practitioners. I'd come full circle—from a patient enduring a catastrophic accident to becoming a member of a healthcare cohort.

Despite her encouraging words, I still harbored some deep-seated doubts. "This computer stuff really overwhelms me," I confessed to a classmate who was my daughter's age. "I'm not sure I'm cut out for nursing. This is so tough at this stage in my life. I wonder if it's too late to embark on a new career."

"You can learn this, Sheryl. I'll be happy to assist you in navigating the digital world," she said. Her guidance was a lifeline through a sea of technological confusion. We began to meet frequently, and I slowly began to figure out the complexities of modern technology. She explained things in a way that made sense to me, she increased my confidence, and she taught me practical skills I needed to know.

Soon my advisor asked me to choose the location for intensive hands-on training, a decision that would shape my nursing experience. "I'd like to be assigned to the burn unit where I once was a patient."

She raised an eyebrow. "Nobody has ever requested that area for their practicum; in fact, I would never have suggested it to any student for their first intensive because it's a tough place to work.

You'll encounter people with catastrophic injuries there who are in tremendous pain. Some may even die."

"As a former burn patient, I realize that. I have much to give back." At the same time, the thought of returning to that floor was bittersweet. I knew it would bring back painful memories of the struggles I'd endured. But I believed I'd be in a special position to lift up those who were on the same journey recovering from the burns that I'd suffered over thirty years ago. My advisor approved my request.

My first day at the burn center was surreal. When I walked through those familiar doors, everything felt both foreign and intimately familiar. The chemical smell was overpowering. It stung my nostrils as soon as I entered the unit, reminding me of my surgeries. The sounds of carts rolling down the hallways reverberated while I traversed the fluorescent-lit corridors, the clatter of wheels on linoleum, a steady background noise that never seemed to fade. Monitors beeped incessantly, raising the specter of being hooked up to IVs like I had been as I teetered between life and the unknown. The incessant rhythm brought back a flood of memories.

The first patient I was assigned to work with was a gentleman about my age with burns over more than 75 percent of his body from an electrical explosion. His bedside nurse told me that he'd recently been resuscitated following a cardiac arrest. Preoccupied with another patient, she asked if I could check on him to ensure everything was all right. As I headed toward his room, I recall thinking, "Gosh, what am I expected to do?"

I approached his motionless form. A wave of helplessness washed over me. The wires and tubes that were connected to him branched out from a monitor beside his bed, forming a complex network of medical machinery that was sustaining his life. The sight evoked memories of when I was tethered to a monitor for weeks, fighting for my own survival. An oxygen mask concealed his face, and his features were indistinct, giving him an almost ethereal appearance. His chest rose and fell rhythmically in sync with the ventilator that controlled his breathing, in contrast to the stillness of his unconscious state. Suddenly, the monitor emitted a loud beep. I panicked. I needed to get help. Rushing to the nurses' station, I urgently requested that someone come to assess his condition.

When I followed the nurse back into his hospital room, a wave of lightheadedness washed over me. My training hadn't prepared me to face someone in such a dire condition. The air thick with the pungent odor of burned flesh evoked memories of how my singed body smelled as I emerged from the burning cockpit. Alarms from the monitors were jarring.

His life was hanging in the balance, and I couldn't tear my gaze away. My thoughts drifted back to when I, too, was perched precariously between life and death, the machines keeping me alive. The scene was hauntingly familiar—even his mother, like mine, sat vigilantly by his bedside. I held myself back from crying out, "Hang on. The fight is worth it." It would draw too much attention. Perhaps they'd think that because I was a burn survivor, I wasn't tough enough.

The intensity of the memories and parallels were too much to bear. I couldn't stay in his room any longer. When I was a burn survivor peer support representative, I was in and out, and hadn't spent extensive time with any patients in peril on the unit. This was very different. Spending an extended time there encountering patients who were on the brink of death brought back my own experiences. I stepped away from the patient's bed to catch my breath and moved toward the door. I had to lean my body against the frame as I felt faint and was unsure if I could walk down the hallway without falling. A woman approached me. When she placed her arm around my shoulder, I recognized her as a nurse who had worked on the unit when I was a patient there. "Sheryl, why are you here? It must bring back so many traumatic memories for you."

Her kindness helped center me. "Patti, I chose to become a nurse because I understand what these patients are going through. I've been there myself, and I want to ease their journey. That's why I'm here."

"You're pale and clammy. I'm not sure this is good for you. I appreciate your motives, but why put yourself through this?" Patti pulled a tissue from her pocket and handed it to me while we stood there quietly for another minute or so. "Let me know if you need anything. I'm here for you. And please take care of yourself." Patti's words reverberated as I went back into the patient's room.

I persisted with my practicum at the burn center. It was an important step in my education, and even more so, I felt it was my calling. This opportunity to use my experience to help others was how I wanted to live the second chance at life I'd been given.

I took four continuous semesters without a break. When we were about to graduate with our Master of Nursing degree, one of my instructors asked me, "Have you thought about applying for the Doctor of Nursing Practice program? I think you should."

Initially I'd been reluctant to pursue further education, but now after completing my master's, I experienced a surge of excitement at the prospect. The Doctor of Nursing Practice, often referred to as a "DNP," would expand my abilities and provide me with greater credibility.

There were considerations that gave me pause. "I know how competitive it is to get into the DNP program. Why would the school want to invest its resources in me at this point in my life? I'm nearly 65 years old."

The instructor countered, "Sheryl, you have such wisdom and lived experiences. I've seen how you interact with other students, watched you work with patients, and heard what you contribute in the classroom. You have so much to offer. Please don't sell yourself short. The Admissions Committee looks at all factors when they decide who gets into the program. I think you should give more thought to submitting an application."

After careful consideration, I realized that obtaining a doctorate in nursing practice would provide me with the opportunity to make a greater impact in the healthcare sector, albeit in a different capacity than I'd originally imagined. A career in bedside nursing at my stage in life wasn't practical. How would I endure grueling all-night shifts, emptying bedpans, and lifting heavy patients? It didn't appeal to me, and these would be the typical responsibilities of a new nurse. I decided to submit my application to the competitive DNP program, holding onto a glimmer of hope that my experience and passion for nursing would shine through and open this new door for me. When I received my acceptance letter in the mail, the news brought a sense of validation and enthusiasm about the future.

When my children were still under one roof, the days were filled with the hustle and bustle of raising a family. Those days passed by swiftly. At times, I wish I'd grasped then just how soon they would be adults and that those treasured days of their youth would never return. In what seemed like a mere moment, they matured. By the time I was accepted into the nursing program, they had all embarked on their academic pursuits, graduated from college, and found the loves of their lives. I came to terms with the past by returning to school myself to chase my unfulfilled dream of being able to more significantly give hope to burn survivors.

The fall of 2014, I began my doctoral studies, diving into the world of advanced nursing with a special focus on Health Innovation and Leadership. In addition to my studies, I'd accepted a part-time position at the burn center as the peer support representative. In this capacity, I spent the next three years at the bedsides of patients, providing encouragement and assistance to them and their families. I also co-led a support group for burn survivors who had been discharged from the hospital—a natural extension of my desire to contribute to the healing process of those in need.

One of the first people I met at the support group was a man who'd been burned on his face and upper torso when he was filling his mower, and the gas can exploded. I'd been meeting with him for over a month before he brought his wife to a meeting. He introduced me to her afterward.

"Remember how I've told you about the meetings Sheryl and I have had? She has been most helpful."

"Yes, of course. I've heard a lot about you. Thank you for helping my husband. He so appreciated that you explained his treatments to him and let him know what to expect next."

During my own experience in the burn unit, I'd learned what not to do, and I recalled often feeling in the dark about what my treatments entailed. Patients deserved to know exactly what the doctors and nurses were doing and what was happening to their bodies. Every patient had my 100 percent support to be an active participant in their own recovery.

After a brief pause, the patient's wife continued, "Tonight you mentioned that you were burned in an airplane crash in St. Paul. We know all about it." I wondered how she knew. My accident had happened more than 30 years ago. "Our home was near where your plane went down. In fact, you almost hit our house."

I was stunned. I felt a deep and instant connection to this woman and her husband. There were so many questions I wanted to ask, but when I opened my mouth, no words came out. Before I could regain my composure, she said, "We were watching TV and we heard a whooshing sound. When we looked out our living room window, we saw your plane go through the trees before it crashed and went up in flames."

I couldn't believe what I was hearing. They witnessed my crash. "We ran outside where your plane went down. Then we saw our priest come out of St. Vincent's and give you last rites. We prayed right along with him." I was so overcome with emotion that I couldn't say anything. I saw God's hand in bringing us together and realized that by helping her husband, I was where I was supposed to be.

That year, my church organized a medical mission trip to Peru. I volunteered to go. While there, I worked at Peru's National Pediatric Burn Center where I witnessed a critical gap in care: the young patients did not have access to any compression garments. In the United States, they had been the standard of care for burn patients since the 1970s to reduce the disfigurement, the visibility, the raised appearance, and the discoloration of scars. I'd benefited personally from wearing the garments on my hands, my arms, my legs, and on my torso for two years, so I understood their importance first-hand. No burn patients in Peru had ever had access to these garments, and, as a result, many faced severe scarring from their burns. The disparity of treatment between the U.S. and Peru struck a deep chord within me.

Back at school, all DNP students were required to take on an extensive project, one that not only demanded considerable time and effort but also the publication of a scholarly paper. I was inspired to focus my DNP project on introducing compression garments to the pediatric burn population in Peru. This endeavor aligned with my commitment to give back, especially to those who had experienced burns like my own. My goal was to bridge the gap in care between the United States and the underdeveloped country of Peru. The children there desperately needed and deserved this essential treatment.

But I wasn't sure how or where to get the compression garments.

First, I thought to approach an American manufacturer of the garments to partner with a Peruvian company to produce them in Lima. This seemed to me to be a win-win: the American business would have access to a new market for distributing their products and could lower their production costs by using the less expensive labor force in Peru. At the American Burn Association annual trade show that year, I presented my proposal to the owner of a reputable compression garment company located in Ohio. At first, she hesitated. She eventually offered to help in a different way by sending patterns, samples, and fabrics for the garments to Peru, along with instructions for them as to how to measure patients. I would deliver these items to the head surgeon of Peru's pediatric burn center at an upcoming burn conference. The head surgeon could then return to Peru with them. Thrilled with this solution, I spent the next several weeks soliciting contributions of additional materials from other American compression garment manufacturers. I also began to fundraise to help cover the additional baggage fees that would be incurred by the surgeon when she took suitcases filled with these materials back to Peru.

Understanding the critical need for these garments, the National Pediatric Burn Center in Peru made a pivotal decision. They purchased an industrial grade sewing machine and hired a skilled seamstress to produce the compression garments directly at their hospital, using the materials and patterns I had provided. This initiative was a game-changer. Rather than waiting for a full-scale manufacturing partnership to be established between an American company and one in Lima, they could set up production right then and there in Peru.

Before long, the impact of our combined efforts became evident. Each child, upon discharge from the burn center, received two sets of these specially tailored garments. I was there to witness the fittings of the first batch on the children. It was profoundly moving. Despite the pain and suffering from their burns, the hope in their eyes was unforgettable. More than just a medical necessity, it was transformative for these young patients, improving their physical and psychological recovery significantly.

The success of the project exceeded my expectations. We'd provided vital medical supplies and created a sustainable solution that directly addressed the needs of burn survivors in an underdeveloped country. Its success sparked broader discussions on elevating burn care standards in Peru and other countries with few resources. My scholarly paper, *One World, One Standard of Care*, discussed the potential for transforming the recovery of burn patients worldwide and improving their quality of life, if only advanced countries would share their resources with developing countries. Most importantly, it showed how the efforts of one person could impact many lives in a distant country.

With my coursework, the DNP project, and my publication behind me, I graduated alongside over 300 others who had also earned their Doctor of Nursing Practice degrees.

It was a significant moment for all of us. In the lead-up to the graduation ceremony, the DNP graduates were given the opportunity to nominate a fellow student to speak at the event to represent all of us. The choice would be made by the nursing school's faculty and administration, keeping their decision secret until graduation.

To my utter surprise, I received word that I'd been selected for this prestigious honor. It was the perfect opportunity to publicly thank the school, my classmates, and my cohort for the profound impact the program had on my life and for the many lessons I'd learned. I chose not to tell my family beforehand to enjoy their surprise firsthand when they saw me onstage at the ceremony. All the graduates, dressed in caps and gowns, made their way into the auditorium. Seated in the audience, my family searched for me among the sea of graduates, unaware that I was seated on stage, positioned between the head of the University of Minnesota Board of Regents and the Dean of the School of Nursing, and with the other dignitaries scheduled to speak.

Waiting for my turn to address the audience, I reflected upon my journey through the DNP program. The hard work, challenges, triumphs, and invaluable lessons learned led to my earning a DNP degree, and I hoped I inspire my fellow graduates to look for opportunities to give back as we embarked on our next chapters.

After graduation, I continued my mission of service by taking a senior leadership role at a Minneapolis hospital for low-income patients. The position enabled me to make an impact on the underserved in our community. I then entered academia to train future nurses. Guided by a deep-seated desire to reciprocate, each step on my way has been profoundly shaped by my own experiences. The journey has become my identity. By giving to others, I have received immeasurably more.

International medical mission work became a new path for my life to make an impact in underdeveloped countries. Here are a few ways that I volunteered my time. During two trips to Kenya, I worked at a clinic in a school and home for abandoned and abused girls. Our visits not only provided immediate medical assistance; they nurtured hope and resilience in these young girls. During a trip to Uganda, we distributed eyeglasses to individuals who had never had access to proper vision care. Their sheer wonder when they donned glasses for the first time filled me with great satisfaction. On an expedition to Honduras, our medical team focused on identifying people with significant blood pressure problems. We were able to emphasize the critical need for basic health screening and education, as well as to refer those needing further care to a nearby hospital. When I worked with young burn survivors in Peru, I witnessed their courage and the transformative power of medical care. The physical healing of every bandage changed, each wound carefully treated, delivered a message of hope—their futures could still be bright despite the shadows of their pasts.

I returned from each trip with uplifting memories and with the realization that my actions, however small they seemed, could ripple across communities and countries. On each step of this journey, from the bustling clinics abroad to the quiet bedside visits in local burn units, I've observed that empathy is a force just as potent as medicine, a listening ear can be as healing as a surgical hand, and small acts of kindness go a long way in life.

Looking back, I've come to terms with the fact that the past is set in stone. In hindsight, if given the chance to relive my life I wouldn't change much. The past has laid a foundation of wisdom and resilience upon which I can build the next chapter of my life. As my children now nurture families of their own, I hope they realize that under the circumstances, I gave them all the love and attention I possibly could. The magnitude of my dedication to them knows no bounds. My focus now remains on making the most of the present and future, ensuring that I'm the best parent and grandparent they could ever wish for.

We humans all have personal goals. But I've learned life takes on a deeper dimension when we assume responsibility for people less fortunate than ourselves. Every moment I spend providing assistance to others confirms that I was afforded a second chance in life to help restore others. It is not just what I do—it defines who I am. Now, more than ever, the legacy I hope to leave behind is to make a tangible difference in the world by giving back, one person at a time.

Graduation from University of Minnesota Master of Nursing degree at age 63

I worked at the Burn Center while getting my Doctor of Nursing Practice degree from 2014 to 2017

Sheryl Ramstad

GRATITUDE FOR A NORMAL LIFE

Sheryl Ramstad with Candyce Kuehn, RN, the Burn Center's nurse manager. Kuehn was one of Sheryl's nurses in 1979.

Experience as Burn Center patient inspires judge to become nurse

In October 2012, Sheryl Ramstad gave up her position as a judge on the Minnesota Tax Court to pursue a master's degree in nursing from the University of Minnesota. As part of her educational requirements, she asked to spend a semester working as a nurse at the Burn Center at Regions, where she was a patient 34 years ago. "I feel a deep debt of gratitude to the Burn Center for saving my life," Sheryl said.

Sheryl was an assistant U.S. attorney in July 1979 when the plane she was flying crashed in St. Paul. She was in the middle of her first solo flight when the plane's engine quit. By all accounts she did a heroic job landing while keeping others out of harm's way. Sheryl broke

out of the burning plane but suffered severe burns to 37 percent of her body, including her hands, arms, back and legs.

The St. Paul Fire Chief arrived at the scene and asked Sheryl where she wanted to go for care. According to Sheryl, "He said that one of the best burn units in the country was a few miles away," at what later became Regions Hospital. "I said 'Please take me there.'"

Sheryl had seven surgeries during her seven weeks in the Burn Center. "Working with burn patients is challenging," Sheryl said, speaking from her experience as both a patient and nurse. "A patient's life is in the

I returned to the burn unit to give back

> "I feel a deep debt of gratitude to the Burn Center for saving my life."
> —Sheryl Ramstad

balance every day they are recovering from a burn. It's not just the burns that make a person vulnerable. In my case they had to watch for pneumonia and lung damage. There's also the risk of infection, internal problems and psychological trauma. Burn care requires a special expertise and focus possessed by the Burn Center's staff."

"A lot has changed since I was a burn patient," Sheryl said. "In no small part that's the result of burn centers using research to improve care. Regions specifically has an international reputation for cutting-edge burn innovations that have saved lives."

One thing that has not changed over the years has been the compassion of Burn Center staff. Several of Sheryl's own care providers — including three nurses, a doctor and a physical therapist — still worked on the unit in 2013, when Sheryl did her clinical rotation. "It brought back memories of my own hospitalization," Sheryl said. "The staff gave me a lot of encouragement back then."

Sheryl remembers one attendant who would stop to brush her hair when she was hospitalized. A Burn Center nurse challenged Sheryl to run Grandma's Marathon in Duluth two years later. Sheryl fulfilled that goal and has completed seven marathons since her accident.

Sheryl earned her master's degree in nursing in December 2013 and wants to work with burn patients. She also plans to pursue a doctorate in nursing practice. "Because of the staff in the Burn Center I've had 34 years of normal life. Each year on my birthday I reflect on how lucky I am."

BURN CENTER CELEBRATES 50th ANNIVERSARY

Tony Gonzalez (second from left) participated in the 2013 BurnAid Golf Classic, which benefited the Burn Center at Regions. He is pictured with (from left to right) Dave Davis, Christine Pulkrabek, Jerry Bradley and Mark Gonzalez.

In 2013, the Burn Center at Regions Hospital celebrated 50 years of internationally-recognized burn care excellence.

Tony Gonzalez can personally attest to the quality of its care. In 1997 he suffered second- and third-degree burns over 95 percent of his body in a propane gas explosion. Tony spent nine months in the Burn Center, where he underwent a number of surgeries, physical therapy to learn to walk and talk again and psychological therapy to deal with the trauma of the accident. "I couldn't have asked for better care, both for myself and my family," Tony said.

Since his accident, Tony has become involved in burn care efforts nationwide, speaking at the World Burn Conference, attending the national conference of the American Burn Association and visiting hospitals across the country. This includes trips back to Regions. "The care offered in the Burn Center can be put at the highest level," he said.

Tony also became the Burn Center's largest individual contributor. Donations have played a key role in helping the Burn Center become the most complete and extensive facility of its kind in the Upper Midwest. Contributions pay for facility renovations, additional equipment and programs that meet the educational and emotional needs of patients. "Contributing was my opportunity to give back to the Burn Center and burn community as a whole," Tony said. "I feel I can personally move forward in my recovery because the support is there."

Page two of Regions Burn Unit article

EPILOGUE

In the past, people often commented to me that I should write a book about my life. The suggestion has been made in a variety of contexts to address so many aspects of my life—surviving an airplane plane crash, pursuing public service as a prosecutor and a judge, running marathons, adopting children from another country, overseeing prisons, serving in the Governor's Cabinet, campaigning for a political office, summiting Mt. Kilimanjaro, attaining master's and doctorate degrees at the age of 62 , and beginning a new career after nearly 45 years as a lawyer. My reply, often said in jest, was always, "I'm too busy living my life to write about it!"

This cryptic retort masked a deep reluctance, a hesitation to pause and reflect on a journey that was still unfolding.

Now that I've passed the milestone of turning 70, and I no longer have full-time employment for the first time in half a century, I've had the time and opportunity to reflect upon what a full life I've had. During what some have whimsically described as a time of "retirement," or while trying to live a meaningful life in my aging years, a stark realization dawned on me: If not now, when?

What a ride it has been! The task of sifting through decades of memories has been both exhilarating and exhausting, a reminder that life made indelible marks on my psyche. One couldn't describe my life as straightforward, uncomplicated, or smooth sailing; it has been packed with bumps, hiccups, and detours. But every single challenge, every stumble, was a hidden gift, a nudge toward understanding myself and the world a bit better. I'd like to invite the reader to join me on my voyage, to traverse the landscapes of a life lived with intention, passion, and an insatiable desire for adventure. My reflections are intended to serve as a source of inspiration and encouragement for those who may be stalled in their own journeys or who are fearful of their next steps.

Writing a memoir is not about achieving perfection or providing a neatly-packaged work. Instead, it is the continuous act of living and learning that imbues our stories with meaning and connects us to each other. I've sought to convey not only the highlights and triumphs, but also the mistakes, the regrets, and the lessons learned along the way. I've grappled with the malleability of memory—how recollections can be colored by emotion, distorted by time, or influenced by subsequent events. Memories, after all, are not infallible records but rather, interpretations of experiences. I acknowledge the subjective nature of my memory. Striving for accuracy, I've consulted with friends and medical staff, and I have reviewed old diaries, letters, articles, photographs, and other memorabilia, seeking to anchor my narrative in tangible evidence of the past. Alongside this truth, there's also a good deal of innocent misremembering.

In sharing my story, I aspire to illuminate the human experiences that transcend individual differences. I am not just recounting my life but invite others to reflect on the universal themes of love, loss, resilience, and redemption that resonate in us all. In the moments when I felt most exposed and raw, I forged my deepest connections. Scars do not define people; rather they are defined by their ability to get up after a fall, emerging stronger from the trials endured. Through shared struggles, I found solidarity and understanding, binding me to others. These lessons, hard-earned and through tears and determination, infused me with the courage to face forward—ready and excited for whatever the future would hold. I hope this book inspires others to look at their lives as an ongoing journey of the continuous act of living and learning. Then it will have served its purpose.

Throughout life, faith has been my compass. It showed me the power of belief—not just in a higher power, but in the goodness within each person and the potential for redemption and renewal—reminding me that even in the darkest times, there is light to be found, if only we seek it. My family and friends have been my anchor, providing love, support, and a sense of belonging that have enriched my life beyond measure. They have taught me the unbreakable bonds that form when we share our lives, our dreams, and our fears with those we love. These relationships have been a mirror, reflecting to me the best parts of myself and challenging me to grow, to forgive, and to love more deeply.

As I inscribe these closing thoughts, I do so with a sense of completion, yet also with the anticipation of new beginnings. I am buoyed by the belief that the best chapters in my life remain to be written. The past has laid a foundation upon which I can build the next chapter of my life. I may not know what twists and turns lie in wait; however, I carry with me the lessons of the past—not as burdens, but as beacons of light guiding my way. The road ahead is filled with infinite possibilities, and I step into the unknown with a spirit of exploration, eager to embrace whatever comes my way. My story is a bridge to the future, and I hope an invitation to others to find their own path of purpose and passion.

And so, with a heart full of dreams and eyes fixed on the horizon, I'm looking forward to the wonders that await. I am not simply hopeful for the future; I'm charged up for it!

ACKNOWLEDGMENTS

Throughout my life, I have been blessed with an abundance of riches, chief among them my family of origin. From my parents, Marvin and Della Mae Ramstad, and my dear older brother and only sibling, Jim, I gleaned the fundamental values that have shaped my character and guided my journey. Their legacy of valuing familiar bonds, providing unwavering loyalty, and giving me boundless love laid the groundwork upon which I have built my life. Their teachings extended beyond the confines of our home, emphasizing the importance of integrity, service to others, and active citizenry in the community, state, and nation.

Their examples of generosity and steadfast faith illuminated my path and inspired me to strive for excellence in all of my endeavors.

My husband, Lee Larson, stands as a pillar of strength who's had abiding faith in me. Throughout the arduous process of penning my memoir, his support and encouragement have kept me going and have provided me with the fortitude to persevere through moments of doubt and uncertainty.

My children—Sarah, Charlie, and Kristina—and their spouses—Brian, Brittany, and Jordan—have greatly enriched my life and given it meaning. They believed in my abilities, forgave my mistakes, and bolstered my resolve, infusing each word with renewed purpose and determination. My love for and devotion to them knows no bounds. And their children—my six grandchildren—Evelyn, Marvin, Savannah, Lorelai, Corinne, and Heather—are the light of my life and give me hope for the future.

Writing a memoir is a journey not to be traversed alone. Sarah Cassidy, my writing companion whose presence has been a source of immeasurable strength and inspiration, stood in my corner. I also have been blessed with dear friends, some of whom have been by my side throughout the experiences described in this memoir—Mary Muehlen Maring and Pat Miles. Without their support, I wouldn't have been able to write it.

I owe a great debt of gratitude to my editors, Mary Balice Nelligan and Janet Horvath, who collaborated with me in making my memoir a reality, breathing life into its pages. I appreciate how Mary engaged with me on this extensive and involved process, helping me translate concepts and memories into a tangible form. And I am grateful for Janet's ongoing support as she shaped and developed the narrative.

Last, but by no means least, I recognize the valuable role of my publishers, Patti Fors and Audrey Fierberg of Muse

Literary. Initially, writing the memoir was just an idea I discussed with them. Had it not been for their enthusiastic assistance, this book would not have been completed.